PRAISE FOR
WHERE **HOPE SEEMS** IMPOSSIBLE

Thanks to these wonderful young poets, so brave to speak out and share their lives—what they say offers great hope in a deeply troubled time. Through tender, thoughtful lines, we are reminded what honesty feels like. We come away touched by our new friends, and inspired.

– Naomi Shihab Nye
(Emeritus) Young People's Poet Laureate

This anthology speaks with a clarity, courage, and urgent tenderness that refuses to be quelled. These young writers bear witness to pain and survival. However, above all else, we see unflinching hope in their words. Every poem reminds us that the voices we most need to hear are already speaking. We simply have to listen.

– Katerina Canyon
Poet, Pushcart Prize-nominee,
Executive Director of Peace Economy Project

WHERE HOPE SEEMS IMPOSSIBLE

A Pongo Youth Poetry Anthology

OTHER **BOOKS** BY **PONGO** PUBLISHING

The Story of My Heart (2021)

The Shadow Beside Me (2020)

Above the Waters of My Sorrows (2015)

There Had to Have Been Someone (2011)

Love is Like All the Colors of the Doors in Juvie (2007)

How Tucked in the Corner was Sadness (2005)

My Passion Leaps Out Toward the World (2005)

Because I Didn't Know the True Meaning of Love (2004)

See What Goes on Behind My Masks (2003)

I Lost My Sense of Protection (2001)

No More Me (2001)

What Every Guy Tells Me (2000)

Trapped in the Ghetto (1999)

I Can't Imagine Myself Any Other Place (1998)

House on the Corner II (1997)

House on the Corner I (1993)

WHERE HOPE SEEMS IMPOSSIBLE

A Pongo Youth Poetry Anthology

FALL 2020–SPRING 2024

FOUNDER: Richard Gold

CO-EXECUTIVE DIRECTOR, DEVELOPMENT & FINANCE: Nebeu Shimeles

CO-EXECUTIVE DIRECTOR, PROGRAMS: Ashley Skartvedt

PROJECT LEADS: Aisha Al-Amin, Sergej Buchholz, Emily Holt, Nico Hwang, Shaun McMichael, Arlene Naganawa, Paige Reischl, Lylli Srygley-Meredith, Kieanna Stephens-Sorn, Ann Teplick

POETRY MENTORS: Michael Barrett, Maggie Black, JoJo Bromfield, Tommy Brock, Sam Bunn, Caroline Catlin, Rey Delagarza, Angela Franklin, Sho Glick, Bernie Hall, Hannah Hinsch, Mark Johnson, Lena Kabeshita, Winson Law, Meta LeCompte, Alex Leviton, Kristina Mageau, Emma McVeigh, Karina Quiroz, Rebecca Richards-Diop, Raul Sanchez, Gemlene Schaudies, Lu Anne Simpson, Heather Timkin, Amelia Worley, Irene Yung

PONGO POETRY PROJECT
Seattle, WA, October, 2025

PONGO
poetry project

Copyright ® 2025 Pongo Publishing

All rights reserved.

No part of the contents of this book covered by the copyright herein may be reproduced or used in any form or by any means—including photocopying, recording, taping, or information retrieval systems—without the written permission of the publisher.

The writers contributing to *Where Hope Seems Impossible* retain copyrights on their individual works presented in this volume.

Published in October, 2025, by

PONGO PUBLISHING, INC.
130 2nd Ave N, #3068
Edmonds, WA 98020
www.pongopoetryproject.org
info@pongopoetryproject.org

Book Design: Rebecca Richards-Diop
Editor: Ashley Skartvedt
Consulting Editor: Nebeu Shimeles

Printed and bound in the United States of America

Dedicated to all Pongo Poets

Thank you to everyone who has helped make Pongo Poetry Project and this anthology possible.

We acknowledge all the staff employed at Pongo's direct service sites for their service, particularly those who directly supported Pongo programming from fall 2020-spring 2024, including:

CHILD STUDY AND TREATMENT CENTER
Erin Carpenter, Tausha Goss-Squier, Raewyn Heim, Nick Kirchoff, Kyle Lance, Anna Seiler, Dr. Michael Storck, Dan Sutich, Liz Tarr

CLARK CHILDREN AND FAMILY JUSTICE CENTER
Unna Kim, Karen Kinch, Ashley Mareld, Vanessa Marroquin, Michelle Mihail

ECHO GLEN CHILDREN'S CENTER
Kolanye Bykoff, Emily Choppin, Daniel Gotkin, Allison Illgenfritz, Haley Lowe, Jesse Malone, Lindsay Myatich

A special thanks goes out to all of Pongo's employees, board members, and volunteers, especially our Project Leads and Poetry Mentors listed on the title page. Without your care and dedication, none of this would be possible.

A sincere appreciation is reserved for our first readers, who graciously volunteered their time to review this book: Sergej Buchholz, Arlene Naganawa, Lylli Srygley-Meredith, and Ann Teplick.

Finally, thanks to the following grantors for their generous support of Pongo programming and the young people we serve:
4CULTURE; ARTSFUND; THE ALLISON FOUNDATION; BECU; THE BELLA ARTS FOUNDATION; CHARLOTTE MARTIN FOUNDATION; CITY OF SEATTLE, OFFICE OF ARTS & CULTURE; FALES FOUNDATION TRUST; THE FLORENCE B. KILWORTH FOUNDATION; FOUNDRY10; HELEN MARTHA SCHIFF FOUNDATION; THE IBIS FOUNDATION OF ARIZONA; THE NORCLIFFE FOUNDATION; THE POETRY FOUNDATION; TULALIP TRIBES CHARITABLE FUND; WASHINGTON STATE ARTS COMMISSION; VIRGINIA MASON FRANCISCAN HEALTH; WINDERMERE FOUNDATION

In order to protect the privacy and confidentiality of the authors from our in-person programming, their names, as well as the names of their family and friends—along with other identifiable details—have been removed or changed. All of the poems remain as close to the original writing as possible, with minimal editing for clarity, consistency, and formatting.

CONTENTS

Dearest Reader 1

CHILD STUDY AND TREATMENT CENTER
Our Days Are Special Like a Birthday 5
I Don't Really Know What's on My Heart Today 6
A Toy Like Me 7
I Am Beautiful, I Was 8
The Blood That Thorns Draw 9
Forgiveness 10
Nectar 11
Finding Air 12
Shaken Soda 14
A Sign of Growth 16
My Discharge is Coming 17
To My Best Friend 18
Losing My Other Half 19
My Heart is No Longer... 20
Cold Nights on I-90 21
Thoughts on Pongo from CSTC Youth 22
Reflections from Pongo Mentors 23
Thanks for Nothing 24
A Cold Sun 26
Paint Me without the Bad Things in My Life 28
Fire vs. Truth 29
If I Had a Blessing Wand 30
Peace 32
When I Think of Home 33
A List Poem...or Not 34
What it Means to Improve 36
Tunnel Brain 38
Faces of Home 40
Reflections from Pongo Mentors 41
Pongo's Fill-in-the-Blank Writing Activity: *Like Me* 42

CLARK CHILDREN AND FAMILY JUSTICE CENTER

Blank Canvas 47
Where I'm From 48
Incarcerated and Scared 50
Back at Home 51
Being in Juvie 52
5 Senses 54
Voice of a Man 56
A Militia Soldier Like Me 58
Sorry Mama 59
Dough 60
Take 61
How I Feel 62
Thoughts on Pongo from CCFJC Youth 64
Reflections from Pongo Mentors 65
The Way Anger Affects Me 66
Anger 67
Where I Am From 68
Not Your Victim 70
Butterflies 72
The Fall 73
Running 74
The Softest Pillow 75
If My Body Could Speak 76
My Other Half 78
The Missing Puzzle Piece 79
Curiosity 80
Looking out the Window While Driving 82
Dear Mom 83
Central District 84
A Revolution for You and Me 86
Reflections from Pongo Mentors 87
Pongo's Fill-in-the-Blank Writing Activity:
Where I Come From 88

ECHO GLEN CHILDREN'S CENTER

Unspoken Ideas 93
Where I Come From 94
Where I Am 96
I Am 97
The Things You Go Through in Life 98
Story of My Life 100
Walk One Mile...in My Shoes 101
Teaching Me and My Brothers to Swim 102
Running 104
Thoughts on Pongo from Echo Glen Youth 106
How I Found Joy 108
My Dog 111
Resentment 112
Tired of the Pain 114
Stay Strong 115
Open Minded 116
Changing Ways 117
Discovering Love 118
My Brothers 119
The Journey to the Future 120
Reflections from Pongo Mentors 121
Pongo's Fill-in-the-Blank Writing Activity: *Running* 122
Youth Poetry Film Shorts 124

WELL-VERSED ONLINE

An Incomplete Puzzle 127
Font Persona 128
Unspoken Weight 130
Swan Lake 131
Shell 132
Myself: Revised Edition 134
I Remember 136
What They Were Wearing 137
I Just Thought You Should Know 138
A Poem About A Dead Girl 140
Thoughts on Pongo from Well-Versed Youth 142
Where To From Here? 144
Reality 145
Rice on a Rollercoaster 146
What We Carried 148
A Palestinian Mother 150
What Is Love? 151
I Hate You out of Love 152
A Taste of Intimacy 154
Thoughts on Pongo from Well-Versed Youth 155
Mamba Mentality Vol.2 156
Seventeen Forever 158
Pongo's Fill-in-the-Blank Writing Activity:
I Just Thought You Should Know 160
About Well-Versed 162

How to Get Involved 163

DEAREST **READER**,

Welcome to the world of Pongo Poetry Project! Whether this is your first time visiting or you've adventured here many times before, you are an accepted member of our community. Pongo is an environment where we encourage you to write from the heart about who you are as a person. It's a supportive, nonjudgmental, and creative space where young people who have experienced adversity, particularly childhood trauma, can feel seen, heard, and affirmed.

This year marks Pongo's 30th anniversary as an organization, and in honor of the occasion, this anthology includes poems written by youth across all of our programming. Each of the first three sections presents a collection of poems written by systems-impacted youth at our direct service sites, including juvenile detention centers and residential psychiatric hospitals in the Seattle area. At each of these sites, a team of trained mentors provides weekly one-on-one poetry writing workshops using the Pongo Method, our trauma-informed, evidence-based, healing-centered approach.

In these workshops, youth are invited to share their stories and express themselves. Our non-hierarchical, youth-driven techniques allow the youth to be in control of their narratives and guide us through the expedition of their lives. They often share the most traumatic events that have happened to them, such as neglect, abuse, and the death of a loved one. However, they also share their deepest desires—like who they love, what they dream about, and how they hope for a better future, which is what inspired the title of this book, *Where Hope Seems Impossible*, after a line from the poem, "A List Poem...or Not" (page 34).

At the end of each writing workshop, we invite the youth to sign a release form, which gives Pongo permission to publish their work anonymously. Because these young people are minors confined to institutional settings, we intentionally protect their privacy and confidentiality by removing names and any other identifiable information from their poems.

The final section is a collection of poems written by youth from around the world who have submitted to our online program, Well-Versed. In this program, one of our dedicated volunteers reads and responds to each submission of poetry on a weekly basis. Selected poems are published on our website and highlighted on our social media quarterly, and one poem is chosen for the annual Pongo Poetry Prize. In their poetry, youth openly share their voyage through their hopes, dreams, fears, and regrets without ever meeting the person on the other side of the screen.

Pouring your heart onto the page, like the young people we serve do, takes vulnerability. In order to be vulnerable you must also be brave. This anthology celebrates the bravery it takes for each of these young people to not only share their story with us, but with you and the world. Please do these young folks the honor of carefully reading their stories and sharing them with the people in your communities. Additionally, we invite you to join the creative process by making use of the fill-in-the-blank writing activities included at the end of each section, the very same activities we use to spark youth self-expression in our workshops. Thank you for your vulnerability and bravery in joining us on this journey. We hope you enjoy traversing the hills and valleys this anthology has to offer. For more information on Pongo and ways to help carry out our mission, please see "How to Get Involved" (page 163).

In Community,
Ashley Skartvedt
CO-EXECUTIVE DIRECTOR, PROGRAMS
PONGO POETRY PROJECT

FINDING AIR

CHILD STUDY AND TREATMENT CENTER

Lakewood, WA
Fall 2020–Spring 2024

The Child Study and Treatment Center (CSTC) is the only state-run residential psychiatric hospital for youth in Washington State. Pongo has provided trauma-informed poetry workshops for youth residing at the hospital since 2000.

241 YOUTH SERVED

CSTC

THE POEMS INCLUDED IN THIS SECTION WERE WRITTEN BY YOUTH DURING PONGO PROGRAMMING BETWEEN THE FALL OF 2020 AND SPRING 2024.

100%
of youth writers enjoyed the Pongo writing experience

98%
OF YOUTH WRITERS WERE PROUD OF THEIR POETRY

89%
intend to write more during future life difficulties

OUR DAYS ARE SPECIAL LIKE A BIRTHDAY
BY A YOUNG PERSON AT CSTC

Birthdays are for celebrating your life
And the fact that you are alive.
Some people might not want their birthday to come
Because they may think that
Getting older means
Leaving your childhood behind.
Even though we all get older,
We all have a child inside us—
A child that may still
Throw a fit when we don't get what we want
Or get too excited over the little things.
That child inside us
Is there no matter how old we get.
Just because we turn 18,
Doesn't mean we leave our childhood behind
Or grow up immediately.

Dedicated to myself and the child inside me

I DON'T REALLY KNOW WHAT'S ON MY HEART TODAY
BY A YOUNG PERSON AT CSTC

I don't really know what's on my heart today
I kind of feel like an animal coming out of hibernation
like a bear that is coming out
looking around
and is not sure what is going on

A bear that wants clarity about the world
who is rubbing her eyes
still a bit sleepy
and hopes for a good rest of the year
hopes to figure out what's going on
hopes to get back on her feet

A bear that's hungry
a bear that would be happy
if she didn't have to go into hibernation again
because during hibernation
she misses out on what's going on in the world
outside the cave

Dedicated to all the bears in this world

A TOY LIKE ME
BY A YOUNG PERSON AT CSTC

I used to look for a toy that looked like me,
a toy with bluish green eyes and a big nose and very blonde hair
I never found one
So it made me think, Am I not good enough?
I used to look for a toy like me,
hoping for an image of myself that could burp the ABC's
or dance for days and was afraid of a big spider under the bed
But all the toys I found seemed like they were made for skinny girls
Looking and not finding, I felt alone

Sometimes I blamed myself because I wasn't a skinny supermodel
Because I couldn't find a toy like me, I gave up
and developed an eating disorder
But now that I'm older, I see my body as beautiful
because I know I don't have to be the skinniest
I still remember the old days
Now I want to move on and love myself

I AM BEAUTIFUL. I WAS
BY A YOUNG PERSON AT CSTC

I am beautiful.

Once I was afraid to be beautiful.

My eyes are beautiful like milk chocolate
Melting in hot cocoa.

Once I was afraid to see my cat being ran over by a huge truck.

My hair is beautiful like the dark night
Dancing through the shadows.

My skin is colorful like a delicious milk chocolate
Being made into a seven-foot-high statue.

My hands are soft like a fluffy cat
Purring on a soft blanket.

Once I was afraid of the dark because you never know
What's lurking in the shadows.

My heart is sweet like the sweetest of sugar and pastries.

I am afraid to feel what it's like to not have family
Or friends who are around to love you.

I am lonely.

I am still lonely.

I will always be lonely.

Bye bye.

THE BLOOD THAT THORNS DRAW
BY A YOUNG PERSON AT CSTC

society's norms stab at me,
their thorns piercing my confidence,
tearing apart every ounce of love
i ever had for myself.

the blood they draw
turns confidence into criticism,
turns the healthy habits
into ones that slowly kill me,
burns holes of hunger
in my stomach,
unleashing a monster that is never satisfied
because society's thorns
tell me what is beautiful.

they repeat it over and over again,
the thorns
draw blood until
every ounce of life is drained from my body
and i am nothing more
than a skeleton of what i once had been.

FORGIVENESS
BY A YOUNG PERSON AT CSTC

I haven't yet forgiven myself for
My broken heart—
Me not getting enough love
From my family.
I feel like my family doesn't care
About me at all.
It makes me feel lonely and sad
Like a broken picture frame.
I haven't yet forgiven myself for
When my cuts are deep,
Deep like a well,
Like a dead flower
Floating on the evening water.
I'm learning to forgive myself
Even when it's hard.

Dedicated to myself

NECTAR
BY A YOUNG PERSON AT CSTC

The rough hive supplies us with the sweet nectar
That is so familiar to us
It graces us with its smooth thick gooey warmth
We collect the nectar
To create the golden honey
That drips from our lips
Sometimes tangling us into messes we never meant to find
Sometimes giving too much grace to something
That does not deserve our sweetness

Dedicated to the people pleasers

FINDING AIR
BY A YOUNG PERSON AT CSTC

Open doors, watching
My life fall into place

Pieces of a puzzle
Fitting together like they were
Always meant to be

Fighting through the shadows
Dispelling the darkness
The type that fills you

Peace overflowing, seeking light
A well drilled into the earth
Of my mind
That became my reason

I used to wade in the ocean that was chaos
Looking for that next high
The next breath of fresh air
The waves washing over me
While my lungs screamed for relief

Silently drowning anything that
Dared to swim

Peace is the air
The air that allows me
To finally be able to breathe

The freedom seeping into
My veins, filling me
With a rush
I could never seem to find

Peace whispering through
The shadows that plague me

Finding the light
that I was always meant to discover
I was destined to find the happiness within

Open doors, watching
My life falls into place

SHAKEN SODA
BY A YOUNG PERSON AT CSTC

Things happen on the cottage that annoy me
I get annoyed all the time
Every little thing
My head will hurt
And I will feel anxious

If I have a long day
And I'm tired
I'll be short with someone
And they'll ask if I'm mad
At them
And I'll say no
But they keep asking
Which does make me mad

It's like repetitiveness
I feel like crap
Like a bad person
Like people think I'm mad at people all the time
I don't want to be rude to people
People deserve respect
You never really know
What's going on with them

You know those sodas
Shaken up at the store
Shaken and shaken
And they look like any other soda
But it's been through other things

That soda could have been
Thrown to the floor
You never know
That day it could have been
Tossed around
Kicked around
Beaten around
Dragged
Till the bubbles bubble up
And bubbles need to come out
Eventually
And someone does the littlest thing
And then that soda explodes on them
You never know with someone
They could be like that shaken soda
Maybe try to open all soda slowly
So that it can fizz down
And not explode on you
It might bubble up
But the bubbles will go back down
And when you drink it
It's still the same soda that you bought for yourself
It still tastes the same
It still tastes like the drink you wanted
You can approach people like that

A SIGN OF GROWTH
BY A YOUNG PERSON AT CSTC

I've been thinking about
being at past facilities and CSTC
and how it is a sign of growth
because when I was younger
I never wanted to get
treatment or help
because I always thought
I could do everything by myself

Like when I was younger
I was into self-harm
and I always thought I could
solve things myself
without medicine or help

What I appreciate about
the facilities and CSTC
is giving me this treatment
because some people aren't even
lucky enough to get it

I appreciate that they give me a realization
that it sometimes takes more people
to get the support you need
because when I was younger
I didn't get that support

Because one person
is not strong enough
to hold the world

*Dedicated to everybody who didn't get this treatment
or didn't get the help they needed when they were younger*

MY DISCHARGE IS COMING
BY A YOUNG PERSON AT CSTC

My discharge is coming
I don't know how to express how I feel
I went to more than 4 facilities
and every one of them I felt excited to leave
I built a better relationship with staff here
than with my own family
My relationship with my family is strained
I can't remember the last time I smiled
or I laughed with them
I was always in facilities or in the hospital
Some of the staff here understand me
They crack jokes and
when they hug me
I feel an emotion that I never
really experienced...
Love

TO MY BEST FRIEND
BY A YOUNG PERSON AT CSTC

For my best friend who is always there for
Me, to brighten my day. To all the
Days we shared, good or bad. Cheers to all the laughs, to all
The tears. When she walks into a room, it's as if she is
There to lighten our mood. I feel terribly guilty
For leaving her behind like that. I wish
I was here with her right now. She is
About to be 13. I hope that I get to see
Her on her big day. Ever since we were little,
She has always been the light to my shadow.
She always knows what to say to make
Me feel better. She is kind and loving.
And our love is worth it. And I
Promise to love her, till the day I die.
But if there is one thing I've learned, it's that: Love
Can be as easy as counting to 3. It can be as hard as
Trusting someone new, but it's worth the amount of love
You are given.

LOSING MY OTHER HALF
BY A YOUNG PERSON AT CSTC

when death comes suddenly
you chase it
it grabs you
it rips the air from your lungs
drowning you in its darkness

on a sunny day
the sky turned grey
the flashing lights
filled my mind

i heard the sirens
i smelled the sanitizer
i touched his cold grey hand
i felt my joy
my light, my life
slip away the moment
that line lay straight

Dedicated to NL

MY HEART IS NO LONGER...
BY A YOUNG PERSON AT CSTC

My heart is broken
It has been since being brought to the light of this world
My heart is scarred, torn, and beaten darker than the night sky
My heart is swirling with pain and hatred,
leaving no room for joy and love
My heart is empty filled with webs
and dust left from time of unease
My heart was gone until I met you
My heart is no longer broken,
my pieces placed together by glue
My heart is no longer starved,
wounds from suffering of time have lifted like a warm breeze
My heart is no longer angry,
it rings forth with choirs of passion and ecstasy
My heart is no longer deserted
but full of our joy
My heart is whole, your pieces complementing mine,
finishing the puzzle of my life

COLD NIGHTS ON I-90
BY A YOUNG PERSON AT CSTC

As I look out the frost-covered window
of the half-working rickety car
I wonder, How did I get here?

When I was younger
my parents were together
but never together

My mom had extended stays at the hospital
that seemed like eternities to a 6-year-old
and my dad chose not to be around
whether or not she was here

When he was around though
time seemed to slow
and moments of pain seemed to grow

It seemed that he chose
the sensations of his own pleasure
over the safety and happiness of the children
that he willingly brought into this world

I swore to myself
that I would never look into a mirror and see
the face of my father on my own
I would never
make the mistakes that he did

Now as I drive home from therapy brought on
by these pains of the past
I look out the window as the sky darkens
and I see his face looking back at me

THOUGHTS ON PONGO FROM CSTC YOUTH

"Before I went to Pongo I was scared to let my feelings out. I felt like I was going to be judged. I felt more comfortable sharing with Pongo. It helped me feel better."

"I like Pongo because I get to express my feelings."

"[Pongo] made me realize I could voice all my words on paper. I've written stories, poems; I share them with people I trust."

"As a poetry mentor with Pongo, I have had the opportunity to witness profound moments of creative joy. I have watched words be transfigured into a healing balm that allows youth whose pain often confounds language to voice that pain and experience a deep sense of relief and accomplishment. There really is nothing like the feeling of lightness and release experienced vicariously through the intimate collaboration of the mentorship process. The youth have taught me the practice of deep listening as well as the value of simply sitting alongside someone who is struggling, having faith that words will come."

– Hannah Hinsch

REFLECTIONS FROM PONGO MENTORS

"It is a strange experience to sit down with someone and invite them to write a poem with you. Many of the youth I worked with had never written poetry, and here are these adults pitching the idea that their honest words were poetry in the making. Again and again I was in awe of these humans. I joined Pongo because I wanted to give youth the gift of knowing that they have something valuable to say and they have the ability to say it powerfully. Publishing this book demonstrates that value to them, and, I hope, to you."

– Sho Glick

THANKS FOR NOTHING
BY A YOUNG PERSON AT CSTC

Dear Y,

You were supposed to love me,
supposed to take care of me,
supposed to intimidate boys
if they ever asked me out,
but you were never around to do that.

Your absence is like me being stranded
on an island,
and no matter how hard
I try to swim and escape,
I never find a way out
and you never show up
to help me.

Whenever I think of a father,
I never think of you.
I never think of what could have happened.
Why bother?
Cuz in the end,
you'll never show up.
It makes me want to ask
Did you ever try? Like, really try?

Because with addiction,
I've had to try.
I've had to work hard.
I've had to wake up in the morning.
I've had to deal with the s***
that life gives you.

But you
just took the easy way.
You don't have to worry
about waking up
and dealing with what life gives you.
I've felt the struggle of wanting to give up
and leave earth,
but in the end,
how can I leave a family
like you left me?

Instead of thanks for nothing,
thanks for showing
me that life is s***. Yet
I'd never leave
those I love.

A COLD SUN
BY A YOUNG PERSON AT CSTC

To my biomom:

You took everything
I needed
and never gave it
back

I needed affection
but you only
hit me

I needed nurture
but you neglected
me

I needed love
but you made it so
I couldn't even love
myself

I needed education
but you wouldn't let
me leave
the house

I needed safety
but you let my siblings
go
unsupervised

I needed comfort
but you caused me
to hide
in my room

I needed friends
but you
isolated me

I needed a mom
but you
wouldn't even
give
that
to
me

You were supposed
to be
my sun
yet I am
still
so
cold.

PAINT ME WITHOUT THE BAD THINGS IN MY LIFE
BY A YOUNG PERSON AT CSTC

Paint me without the bad past
Paint me with a good past and future
Paint me without a broken heart
Paint me as a generous little boy and really loving
Paint me without CPS
Paint me like sunshine and happiness

FIRE VS. TRUTH
BY A YOUNG PERSON AT CSTC

One day I figured out
that my brother died.
Honestly, still, till this day
I don't know why.
I wanted to meet him.
I wanted to see his life,
but till this day I cannot.
And honestly, it hit my heart
in a specific spot.
It's sad, but I couldn't see him, go on
and meet him.
It hits me to where I can't feel anything.
It hits me to where I feel my blood will stop running.
It hits me because I will never know who he truly is.
It hits me because we have the same blood in our veins.
It hits me so bad that I want to turn insane.
I don't know how to feel.
Am I just supposed to let this go?
I just want to go be with him in heaven.
I miss you, brother. Live on.

IF I HAD A BLESSING WAND
GROUP POEM BY YOUNG PEOPLE AT CSTC & POETRY MENTORS

I'd wave it at
my big brother
so that he remembers me

I'd wave it at all the pain and hurt
that no one sees
so that people would more easily
love and heal each other

I'd wave it
at the earth
because this world is cruel
and I want this world to be good

I'd wave it at
people I meet throughout life
so I can help them
right then and there
as I learn about what may
weigh on their heart
and I would hope
my blessing would be a relief

I'd wave it at battlefields
around the world,
so that the people can see
the other people
with their heart
and stop fighting

I'd wave it at the world
so that we all live happy

I would wave it
at the Salish sea
so that the waters are clean
and free of pollution
and filled with salmon
for the orca

I'd wave it at
my mom
to have her happy

PEACE
BY A YOUNG PERSON AT CSTC

I see beauty as waves crashing from the ocean
I see beauty as driving into the sunset
It makes me feel calm
I like to think about my family then
especially my mom
the animals I love
especially my twenty-two cats
and I wish for the world to see
the beauty I see
and it makes me hope that the world
can stay alive as long as possible

I like the birds chirping in the early dawn
I feel happy when I hear their songs
and it makes me want to join their song
and sing about love
and about how grateful I am for
being here
And I would love to sing for my siblings
and my mom
I want them to hear how much I love them
and tell them that I will always be there for them
even when I am not there physically
That is peace for me

Dedicated to everyone

WHEN I THINK OF HOME
BY A YOUNG PERSON AT CSTC

When I think of home,
I think of my room.
It's sea blue.
The only window
Looks out at my neighbor's wall.
Guess that's why they call it
Window pain.*
When I get home,
I'm going to put Christmas lights
Around them—white lights
Like snow falling
And how it sparkles in headlights.
We get wood for the fire—
It makes me feel secure,
Like I'm wrapped in my favorite blanket.
That's what happens when I think of home.

---

* Lines 6 & 7 are inspired by "Love the Way You Lie" by Eminem.

A LIST POEM...OR NOT
BY A YOUNG PERSON AT CSTC

Life can't be listed.
You can't put a list on life.
You can't mark off boxes
for what you want plans to be.
You can't plan for the unexpected.
You might see a happy bright future
or you might see your life being sad
behind bars for the rest of your life
even if the bars are real.
Then there's another set of bars
being prepared for life.
The bar for thinking what you do
and want to do.
Life is tricky,
like wind flown in every direction.
It can send you up to the world's beauty
and it can plummet you
to the dangerous deeps
of the unknown ocean floor
where hope seems impossible.
The thousands of pounds of pressure
keep you down, killing you on the inside.
There is no planning for that.
No box to check off.
A roller coaster of ups
and downs. The flow of the rivers
twists and turns that wind
forwards and back.
In school, you learn everything
you're taught by teachers.
But there's no true teachers.

In life, your life can rise
and fall like mountains.
Life is unpredictable
like earth. You have a choice.
You can make a list and check it off
and be unprepared or flow
like earth and learn from you.
Let earth be your teacher
and have no boxes
or lists to fill.

WHAT IT MEANS TO IMPROVE
BY A YOUNG PERSON AT CSTC

How do I write in a way
That is coherent
About how overwhelmed I am.
I think my room reflects my brain.
It's always been cluttered,
But there's no more dirty dishes.
I'm doing better than I was.
That's probably a phrase I've used quite a lot.

How do you put in words
That improvement isn't always
Just one big line up;
It goes up and down.
Like it's still going up
And it doesn't go quite as far down,
Like a heart monitor
Tracking the way my heart beats.
I mean, it's still beating,
Which is more than I thought I'd be
At this point.

For my whole life, I thought
I wouldn't make it to adulthood.
And well, now I'm here.
I'm not in jail.
I don't have to go back to a psych ward.

Now I'm just left thinking, "Now what?"
Any plans that I made were kind of empty,
Like the bones of a bird's wing
That's just trying to fly.

I didn't think I'd meet any of my goals.
I was just trying to come up with answers
To the question, "Where do you think you'll be
In five years?"
"I don't know, dead in a ditch somewhere."
Even though I'm tired
And I might need breaks,
I will still continue to fly
And reach my destination.
But it might take me a while,
But that's okay.

Dedicated to me in Ketron Cottage, three years ago.

TUNNEL BRAIN
BY A YOUNG PERSON AT CSTC

Hope just kind of comes to mind.
I hope I get out of here.
Hope, simply, is faith in another person
Or something you hope happens.
My family gives me hope.
It feels like positivity,
Their happiness is beaming on me
Like the sun.
The sun is a symbol to people who need hope.
It represents the light at the end of the tunnel.

The tunnel is wet, dark, underground
Where you can't see the sun.
It feels cold.
Certain things are gonna tell you
To give up, and that there's no point,
Or simply that it's hopeless.
That's negative thoughts.
The person saying this could be
Someone that has been bad to you,
That neglected you,
That didn't give you hope.

You could fend them off for a bit
By either stuffing them down
Or coping with them appropriately.
You can talk to someone about it,
Like a therapist or a trusted person.
It's like the tunnel is your mind,
And there will always be someone
Down in there with you,
Telling you to give up.
But there's also another person,
And this person is like the sun,
Who shares their light with you.

Don't listen to the negativity,
Listen to the sun,
And you'll make it.

Dedicated to my mom, thank you
for being my light at the end of the tunnel.

FACES OF HOME
GROUP POEM BY YOUNG PEOPLE AT CSTC & POETRY MENTORS

Home can be many things
To me it can be
The perfect cup of tea where the water comes to a roaring boil
Sitting on the porch in rocking chairs with my grandma
Joking with family
My parents trying to make me eat meat
Even though I'm a vegetarian
What you're passionate about

Home can be many things
Sometimes it can fill you with gratitude like when
My step-brother showed up at the train station to see me off
My friends tell me they care about me
My driveway filled with chalk art
When you see nature surrounding you
When my mom cooks us carbonara

Home can be many things
Sometimes it can make you sad like when
My dad passed away in May this year
You get kicked out of your house
You get things you love taken away from you
When the cemetery is the only place to visit family
When your family doesn't accept you for who you are

Through it all, home to me can be like
A snowstorm
Like Black Friday shopping
A place to just be me
Where I feel welcome
My parents being happy
Still accepting who I am
A reminder we all deserve a place that loves us

"I often feel in awe when we collaborate with the young people at CSTC and discover how much powerful poetry there is inside them: in the many different ways they have held and are now reshaping their stories; in the remarkable insights they have gained; in their struggles, their resilience, and their compassion. All we do is help them turn this inner poetry into actual poems. The process completely flips the tired, seemingly predetermined script for all: They are the ones who become the owners and artists of their stories while we are just lucky witnesses to, and amplifiers for, a stunning, empowering healing experience."

– SERGEJ BUCHHOLZ

❝ REFLECTIONS FROM PONGO MENTORS ❞

"Mentoring with Pongo at CSTC off and on over the past seven years has been such a meaningful experience. Simply witnessing someone in their creativity — however it shows up — is a profound gift, for both the student and the mentor. Just last week, a poem by a youth I once mentored appeared on the cover of the latest zine. The poem had moved me deeply, and then to see the pride in their face was even more moving. Plus: my very first mentor group from seven years ago still meets to this day to practice creativity together."

– ALEX LEVITON

Pongo's fill-in-the-blank writing activity

Like Me

The poem, "A Toy Like Me" (page 7), was inspired by and written with the help of using Pongo's fill-in-the-blank writing activity on the following page.

Activity Instructions:

A disappointing aspect of childhood can be not seeing yourself reflected in books, media, toys, etc. The purpose of this activity is to explore your feelings in response. Fill in the blanks in the poem activity. Use the words suggested or choose your own words to communicate your thoughts as clearly and powerfully as you can. Feel free to add lines of your own, to remove lines, or to change words to fit your purpose.

Pongo's Fill-in-the-Blank Writing Activity

A _____ Like Me
(doll, action figure, toy, book about someone)

I used to look for a toy like me,

a toy with _____
(brown eyes, dimples, big ears???)

and _____ and _____
(a nice smile, rosy cheeks, stubby legs???)   *(curly hair, cowlicks aplenty, my dad's nose???)*

The absence made me wonder _____
(what's so wrong with me, am I special or am I strange, is everybody just....???)

I used to look for a toy like me, hoping for an image of myself to hold—

a toy that _____
(laughed the loudest, could belch the alphabet???)

and _____ and _____
(danced the longest, could jump rope for days???) *(needed to be left alone sometimes, was afraid of the dark?)*

But all the toys I found seemed like they were made for_____
(kids who were white, skinny, tall, boyish, girly???)

Looking and not finding, I felt_____
(frustrated, bored, alone???)

which made me _____
(go quiet, act out, question myself???)

Sometimes I blamed_____because_____
(God, my parents, society???)

Because I couldn't find a toy like me, I_____
(changed, grew up angry, finally stopped looking???)

Now that I'm older I_____
(see myself as a gift of my own, make my own fun, still look sometimes ???)

because I know_____
(I can give other people joy, lots of kids go through this???)

But I still remember_____
(the kid I was, the looking and not finding???)

and I want_____
(things have to change, to go back in time and tell them...???)

Activity Copyright © 2020 Shaun McMichael

LEARNING TO LOVE

CLARK CHILDREN AND FAMILY JUSTICE CENTER

Seattle, WA
Fall 2020–Spring 2024

The Clark Children & Family Justice Center (CCFJC) is King County's juvenile detention facility. Pongo has provided trauma-informed poetry workshops for youth detained at the facility since 1998.

CCFJC

293
YOUTH SERVED

THE POEMS INCLUDED IN THIS SECTION WERE WRITTEN BY YOUTH DURING PONGO PROGRAMMING BETWEEN THE FALL OF 2020 AND SPRING 2024.

99%
of youth writers enjoyed the Pongo writing experience

97%
OF YOUTH WRITERS WERE PROUD OF THEIR POETRY

99%
intend to write more during future life difficulties

BLANK CANVAS
BY A YOUNG PERSON AT CCFJC

When I was born my heart was a blank canvas. Every person is a paint brush, every interaction is a stroke, and my life is an art piece. Although there are rips from heartbreaks and stains from mistakes, there is a spectrum of bold colors to basic nudes to black and white, expressing nothing but the characteristics of those whom I've been in contact with. Some holes are patched up to resemble growth and acceptance, as others are left open to remind myself that there are always things I simply cannot control, and I have to move on. The further away you stand, the more you'll realize how small the negatives are compared to the positives, as the colors mend together making any blank space so small, they're nearly gone. Some colors fade, and some are painted over, but they can never be erased, leaving you with foggy memories. Half of your colors are fate. The other half is your decision. Whether it's people you come across, or people you chose to be around, your painting will be beautiful. Some may like it, some may not. All art is different and even if your final piece doesn't look like The Starry Night, it should look like the most realistic version of impact that others have on your heart, which is artistically beautiful on its own.

WHERE I'M FROM
BY A YOUNG PERSON AT CCFJC

I'm from a place that's not really safe.
We would never even go outside.
Our house had been shot up multiple times.

Inside was boring. I'd always be at
our grandparents' house,
because they lived
in a safer neighborhood.

I'm from a street where I learned to love
while others dwell and hate.

I'm from a long line of people who reflect
about our past.

I'm from confusion about my future—
it's like a fog over the ocean
because you can't see that far,
only what's right
in front of you.

I'm from laughter over failure.
If you're laughing when you fail,
you know you could have done better,
but you maybe didn't put your all in it.
Or you're trying to block out the disappointment
or put on a front
to other people,
or sugarcoat it.
But you could do better next time.
There'll always be a second chance.

I'm from fear,
especially when I think about my past.

I come from a long line of drugs and alcohol.
I come from experiences like football
in the streets
to shootouts in the park.
I come from hot winters
and cold summers.

And I wish my life would become
a future about my past.

That's where I'd like to be from.

INCARCERATED AND SCARED
BY A YOUNG PERSON AT CCFJC

I'm anxious…it could happen any day. I've received
only good news from the lawyer so far.

I'm scared…scared as a person is scared
of heights. It's my first time being here.

I cry every night like a hungry child would
cry for food. I put on my green sweatshirt
and blink the unfallen tears from my
already red eyes.

A guard opens my cell and escorts me
down the hall. I'm led into a room where
I talk to a woman who is going to represent me.

My palms sweat and I gnaw at my bottom
lip, anxious, nervous…I'm escorted up to court
where the judge waits for me. I look
at her…her blond hair graying
the crinkle around her eyes when she smiles.

She looks at me like I'm a close, old
friend. My attorney asks for release
and it gets denied. It feels like someone
is stepping on my windpipe, making
it hard to breathe. I blink back
hot tears.

I'm led back down to my cell where
I break down crying. The guard asks
me if I'm okay. I don't know how
to respond.

So I go lie down and let the
darkness take me.

BACK AT HOME
BY A YOUNG PERSON AT CCFJC

Here, the doors lock on me.
At home, I lock the doors.

Here, we have watery spaghetti.
At home, spaghetti tastes like love.

Here, it smells like a bleachy hospital.
At home, it smells like my oily dog.

Here, the door feels fake, I expect it to open.
At home, I feel the doorknob.

Here, there's violent screaming,
doors slamming, radios beeping.
At home, quiet.

Here, I see my mistakes.
At home, I see my futures.

Here, I can't play basketball.
At home, I have my own court.

Here, my friends have to pay for calls.
At home, they just have to answer.

BEING IN JUVIE
BY A YOUNG PERSON AT CCFJC

It's cold and dark
when you first go in.
People's looking at you
as an inmate,
like you're a dangerous person.
I get cold and shivers
down my spine.

I can feel anxiety
coming by
when they first
take me in my room.
I feel cold and depressed.
I can only see these white walls
every time I turn.

I can only think to myself,
what have I done to be in here?

I miss being with my family and my friends.
I miss having a hug from my mom, the warmth like a fire.
I miss being outside every day, playing Uno with my friends.
I miss steak with greens.
I miss being around the house playing ball with my dog.
I miss having to sit on the porch and seeing the days go by.

When I'm in juvie
I can't see myself outside anymore.
Judges keep telling me I'm a menace to society
or not a good person,
but I know that I am.
I'm a good person.
I'm a loving person.
I just miss my family and being out.

Now every time I go out of my room I just feel a deep cold.
It feels like winter with frostbite on your hands.
I just sit around the table watching people go by.
It feels like years have passed since I sat down.

I sit around and think about how I miss my family.
Playing games.
Having fun.
Hearing my mom laugh
and my family and my siblings.

I love my life.
I know I'm a good person.

5 SENSES
BY A YOUNG PERSON AT CCFJC

As we know, humans have 5 senses:

touch
taste
smell
sight
hearing

To me, all these senses connect to much bigger memories and stories.

Touch—When I feel a cool breeze, it used to remind me of the wind
circling around me out on the beach, where there was nothing
but the water and woods and all the chaos of the city didn't exist.

Now, the chilly breeze in the middle of the night reminds me
of the hoodies I can't wear, the heater I can't turn on,
and the cold that goes a lot deeper than physical temperature.

Taste—When I taste sweet potato pie, it used to remind me
of the togetherness of the family I hold close
and the homemade desserts my Southern grandmother makes.

Now, it reminds me of the many holidays I'll spend away
from my loved ones and the "extra desserts" that are supposed
to make up for the love we won't be receiving.

Smell—When I smell cleaning products in the morning,
it used to remind me of Sunday, when my stepmom would clean
to R & B and gospel in the morning before church.

Now, it reminds me of the major unit clean-ups that drag
throughout the morning during the times all I want to do
is talk to my loved ones at home.

Sight—When I used to wake up to breakfast in the morning,
it would remind me of the mornings when my mom
would wake me up for school or chores, and even though
I could hear her swearing in the kitchen because she wanted
it to be perfect, I never found a flaw in her meals.

Now, seeing that tray sitting on the sink above my toilet,
I know I'll be spending the majority of my day in my cell.

Hearing—When I used to hear the sounds of a door closing,
it would remind me of mom coming home from work
and me walking into the living room to tell her about
my day and insignificant drama and how she would listen
without judgment over my silly arguments.

Now, it reminds me of the doors I can't open,
the handles I can't unlock,
and a freedom I can't seem to find the key to reach.

VOICE OF A MAN
BY A YOUNG PERSON AT CCFJC

I remember when I was young
I used to try to act like I was grown,
but my voice was high pitched.

When I told my mom, "I'm a grown man.
I'm the man of the house,"
my voice was high pitched and squeaky.
I was trying to yell and stomp my foot
on the ground. She smiled, laughed a little.
I think she said, "Not yet."

She picked me up. We started wrestling.
I think she said, "Alright, grown man,
cook me some food." I made cereal.
She laughed a little. She ate it.
She had a smile on her face and said,
"It's good."

Being a grown man, taking care of the family.
Being a leader, showing them the right path.
I think I am that. My voice is serious.
I always tell my little brothers
in a deep voice, "Do good."

I remind them every day I talk to them,
"Don't wind up in here.
I don't want you to be in my shoes.
Think about Mom." She's a single mom
with five boys. She can't do it all by herself.

I tell my brothers, "Graduate. Go to school.
Put food on the table." I have two older brothers.
One of them works at 7-11. He comes every week
and brings Mom food and money.
His voice is deep, serious.

I think he's a grown man.
He tells me to do right. He tells me,
"Mom's not going to be here forever.
Make sure she's straight. Make her proud.
Walk the stage. Graduate."

A MILITIA SOLDIER LIKE ME
BY A YOUNG PERSON AT CCFJC

I used to look for a toy like me, a toy with brown skin—
a Native American and African American with long hair.
If he were real, would he go through
the same thing I go through?
If he's been through what I've been through
would he take it lightly or harshly?

I used to look for a toy like me,
hoping for an image of myself to hold—
a toy that a friend would need with an open ear
and walk down the long road with me
and explore the world and try different foods.
But all the toys I found seemed like they were made
for kids that don't know much in life
like knowledge, corruption, integrity, and responsibility.

Looking and not finding, I felt I'm all alone
which made me isolate myself from others.
Sometimes I blamed my actions because my emotions
were too hard to bear.

Because I couldn't find a toy like me,
I learned how not to depend on others
and work things out myself.
Learned how to pat myself on the back
when nobody else would.

Now that I'm older I understand that life was full of mistakes.
I have to work hard to get what I want because I know
I'm a very intelligent,
independent
human.

Dedicated to my life as a young'n dumb teenager

SORRY MAMA
BY A YOUNG PERSON AT CCFJC

I'm really sorry for breaking up your family
I'm sorry for constantly stressing you and breaking your heart
I'm sorry for letting you down nonstop
I'm sorry for always having you worry
I'm sorry for always manipulating you every day
I'm sorry for always making your life 100 times harder
I'm sorry for what my addiction put you through

I want to change with all my heart, mind, and soul
It feels like I'm really mature
But the little kid in me always finds a way out at the worst times
I want to be the son you deserve
I want to give you the things in life you deserve
I want to have the mother-son connection we used to have
I want to make you proud
I want you to be grateful that you have a
Son that still cares and loves you for you

You're a great mother, but your family
And the world have let you down too many times
You know I love you and I care for you a lot
I honestly would do anything for you
I may not complete the task
But I will put all my effort into it

I want you to know you're still young
You can accomplish a lot
If you put your mind to it
You've taken care of me
While you were struggling
You made sacrifices for me
I'm grateful that you've been
In my life as long as you have
And haven't given up on me
I hope you can forgive me
For the things I've put you through
You deserve a better son

DOUGH
BY A YOUNG PERSON AT CCFJC

Growing up from under
A household of broken relationships
Gives you a reason to want to
Leave
It's like a puzzle that's missing pieces
Incomplete
Just like my heart

I try and find the good things out of bad situations
But the bad situations are still there
Can never forget that

Growing up in a house of broken relationships
Doesn't give you a reason to
Trust
But it gives you a reason to
Be paranoid
Like walking down a dark alleyway at midnight
With one earbud in your ear

But broken relationships don't mean
That there's no relationship
There's still a relationship
Just beat up
Like dough

When there's a relationship
You can't find it
Easy
To leave
So in that case
You share your broken love
With your broken relationship

TAKE
BY A YOUNG PERSON AT CCFJC

I'm thinking about taking

not giving

I take because

nobody gave to us

I take because

nobody cared for us

We take because

taking has changed us

It made me a bad person

It made me feel no remorse

It made me feel empty-hearted

like an empty garage

that looks abandoned and dusty

worn down and no visitors

It's hard to see how it could be different

I'd like to still be with my family

and stress-free

I'd feel more like my normal self

HOW I FEEL
BY A YOUNG PERSON AT CCFJC

It feels heavy.
Every day that passes by, the days get darker.
You start questioning yourself, your case,
your family. If you'd grown up with more love,
more caresses, I question if things might have been different.
Maybe I wouldn't be here. I might have a different life.
I could maybe be a millionaire. I was always good
at mathematics. I could be an entrepreneur.

I feel calm talking to people. It relieves your stress.
I have the face of my dad. People think I'm angry,
my resting face looks angry to some people.

Sometimes I feel alone, like getting in my own mind.
I'm messed up in all sorts of ways.
My vision gets darker, the lights start dimming
down, the sun goes down.

Sometimes I feel like this is it for me.
Like I'm going to die, the rest of my life here.
I think about my parents and my younger siblings
and they ask why? My mom says she feels
like she lost a piece of her heart.
My grandpa has been crying and it brings me
a lot of pain. My family tries to come see me
when they can.

Today was bad because I felt like I needed
a day to myself because I felt like I needed
isolation even though I don't like it.
I feel like a tornado of conflicting emotions.
Sometimes depression gets me down.

I miss my family so much. There's not a day
I don't break down for them.
At the end of the day, there's not much
I can do. People tell me to be patient.
I'm like in a ball of mystery—I don't know
what street I'm going to go down.
The uncertainty scares me.
I have faith in my savior.
I believe in Allah, the lord almighty.
I read the Quran and God will forgive me
if I have faith. I know that God loves me
no matter what mistakes I made.

I know that people believe in me,
even if don't know them very well.
I worry that there won't be opportunities
for me to get the freedom and love
I need. Most of the time I am afraid
of the situation.

THOUGHTS ON PONGO FROM CCFJC YOUTH

"[PONGO] HELPS ME WHEN I'M FEELING DOWN."

"It was helpful to soothe & calm myself about what I've been going through."

"[Pongo] made me look at writing in a good way."

"It was good and the mentor made it very easy/simple."

"I liked how I was guided through it and not judged."

"[I] just enjoyed taking some time to say a little something about my personal life."

"I'M GRATEFUL FOR THIS WRITING EXPERIENCE."

"What a pleasure to usher a few minutes of self witness and community invocation into an otherwise hard, often lonely place. We mentors are privileged and honored to sit at the table of reflection and vulnerability; assisting in the making of tangible outcomes that outlast our earnest if small efforts."

– IRENE YUNG

❝ REFLECTIONS FROM PONGO MENTORS ❞

"Despite this confined space where fresh, open air is rare, youth here write poetry with breathtaking humanity and creativity."

– WINSON LAW

"During a Pongo session, something new is always created, something magical, a transcendence beyond the confines of the present. It is a privilege and a blessing to sit beside youthful poets, sometimes guiding, sometimes simply recording, as their poems are breathed into life. As Audre Lorde says, 'This is poetry as illumination, for it is through poetry that we give name to those ideas which are, until the poem, nameless and formless-about to be birthed, but already felt.' I am deeply grateful to be present at the birthing of these poems."

– ARLENE NAGANAWA

THE WAY ANGER AFFECTS ME
BY A YOUNG PERSON AT CCFJC

Anger is an emotion that does more harm than good.
Instead of having a simple conversation,
things tend to get out of control.

Anger is a virus that spreads from one place to another.

Anger is an emotion that's always lurking beneath the surface,
and when it comes out it's like a forest fire—
it burns everything.

Angry because I feel like I don't have any control,
and because I didn't have that control,
I couldn't speak up for myself.

Angry because things begin to pile up on top of each other,
like dust on a windowsill.

Angry because court keeps getting pushed back,
because the prosecutor keeps saying he needs more time,
and I think he should have been ready already.
I've been here for a year and a half.

Maybe anger won't always dictate my moves,
like a puppeteer.

Maybe there is a new day for me when I'm released.
I'll get to go back to the park and play basketball.

Maybe anger one day will disappear,
like water down a drain.

Dedicated to my loved ones

ANGER
BY A YOUNG PERSON AT CCFJC

Anger is a blinding force.
My eyes go red.
Physically, anger used in the wrong way
could hurt people.
Everyone has yin and yang—
light and dark.
When I was younger I would tap into
my dark side more.
A part of anger is impulsiveness.
Anger and impulsiveness are brothers
and sisters.
There's other emotions that cause impulsiveness
but anger is the main one.
Whenever I got angry I was very violent.
Mentally anger is a veil in my head
that I have to break through to calm down.
Otherwise, I'll be angry forever.
When anger is rushing through my body
I feel dark and crazy.
I would sit and do nothing to let my anger
ebb away.
Anger is a dark forest burning like hellfire.
But anger will die just like embers in a fire.
But you have to learn to control it.
No one can stay angry forever.

WHERE I AM FROM
BY A YOUNG PERSON AT CCFJC

I am from a street where silence is the start to chaos
The empty dialogue shells
Everyone is waiting for something to happen
Like a long silence before a jump scare

I am from faith in God
To watch over
The little girls
Don't know what they wear
Could change the rest of their lives
The little boys that don't know
That that one cell could give them lice

I am from laughter that rises
Over the cries of broken homes
Screams of hungry babies
And yells of intoxicated fathers

I am from love, and I know that because
While I knew the trauma going on around me
I had family to soothe me
So these elements never touched me

I'm from fear, especially when I think about
Which one of my neighbors will be in a yellow bag next
What little girl will be trapped under a man's body
What innocent boy will lose his life
To a badge and an angered finger

I also come from dedication to do better
Turning losses into motivation
And the will power to break
The invisible shackles I was born with

Because of this, my life will become a place
Of structure for the next generation
A healthy lifestyle
So my younger siblings
Never have to experience what I had to

A place of success through hardships
That seemed impossible
And never ending will power to beat the odds
That's where I'd like to be from

NOT YOUR VICTIM
BY A YOUNG PERSON AT CCFJC

Same story, different girl.
Why'd you go around him? You knew
What he wanted. What were you wearing?
I think the worst part of being a victim
Is feeling like a victim. That word is thrown around.
I think they should be considered survivors.
As if the acknowledgement is a floaty
To pull us out of the water, but the word
Ties around us until someone realizes it's an anchor.
Victim in the eye of the victim:
Not strong enough
Helpless
Exposed
Vulnerable
And most importantly weak.

Because my body was in the hands of someone
I didn't consent to. And I wasn't able to
Defend myself the way I want to.
Because they took so much.
I will not be considered his victim.
Because men have been flawed so terribly
That even my father, the man I used to consider my king,
Let his princess be stolen from her tower.
I will not be his victim.
Although I can no longer feel his body attached to mine,
exploring territory that did not belong to him
and leaving his filth behind,
I will not have the label of being his victim attached to me too.
See me as the person who survived and moved on.
Not the helpless little girl he took advantage of.
I am not his victim.

BUTTERFLIES
BY A YOUNG PERSON AT CCFJC

so beautiful but so delicate
if you watch, the truth of what the butterfly's
been through shows through the illusion
the wings that have flown away from
all her traumas, the anger that burns
like a raging fire in her soul,
the tear that graces her cheek

Butterflies
running from her troubled past
no one sees as she flies into the spider's web
the devil's deal
promising money and happiness
as she tries to wiggle free

Butterflies
so beautiful and so delicate
her beautiful wings hiding so much pain
crumble
she drops to the floor like nothing

THE FALL
BY A YOUNG PERSON AT CCFJC

I almost fell
I almost tried
The little voice in my brain shrieks
No...no...no
My stomach flutters, but it doesn't want to
My eyes are open, but I can't see the future
I could see myself falling & the unknown chasing me
Everything would change & trust would appear
My heart pieces together
My expectation for disaster shrivels
The alarm goes off, I can't go deeper
But I'm pulled in, magnetically, by touch & promise
Just as I'm about to land, my world is shaken
My healing soul divides & shatters
Trust disappears faster than it will ever come
Images flip through my head
& for the millionth time I realize this is why
This is why I don't confide
This is why I don't trust
This is why I can't connect
& everything around me
That makes me feel safe, destroys me
Every pretty wall closes in on me
I am again hit with an ugly truth
When it seems like someone might actually catch you
They drop their hands
& let you fall.

RUNNING
BY A YOUNG PERSON AT CCFJC

Adrenaline
Pumping through my body
Exploding up my legs
Expanding through my fingertips
My body glows
With an electric pulse
A grin
Spreads across my face
As I run
The feeling is euphoric
Can't this be never-ending?

Chasing the feeling gets rough
My glow dims
I feel like I need a re-charge
Tired, like every inch of me is exhausted
Like I've run a 10-mile marathon
Every bone in my body feels like it's melting

I need to find IT again
When I don't have IT I want more
I crave IT like a drug
Every time I get IT, the more tolerance I build
The crazier things I need to do to chase the feeling

Run away
in a way that lets me feel
something

THE SOFTEST PILLOW
BY A YOUNG PERSON AT CCFJC

After yet another day passed
the same softness greets
a mind
a skull in which its contents
are of an exhausted composure.

As the contents are at rest,
the softness embraces the skull,
easing the swollen mind
with comforting compassion,
providing a beautiful
serene embrace around the worn-out mind.

For what rests,
is a delicate conscience which aches,
which longs for the meditation
that it desperately desires
at the end of each and every day.

IF MY BODY COULD SPEAK
BY A YOUNG PERSON AT CCFJC

If my fist could speak, it would tell you all the fights
that I've been through and the things I've shot.
Fights over people trying to take my dignity.
Dignity is big for me and my culture.
Dignity is like a jewel that I put in my heart.

If my feet could speak, they would tell you
how many times I've walked to hell and back.
All the times that I ran away, hoping to chase a better life,
but ending up back in hell.
Hell is like the slaughterhouse
where people get their soul snatched
and where I can't be successful in the way I want,
like being a superhero who can stop all
world hunger and fights and war.

If my eyes could speak, they would tell you about what I've seen
in my life. My eyes feel glossy and hurt from what I've seen,
like a hurricane is blowing and tearing things apart
and I see fear.
Fear of losing my loved ones.
I've already lost a lot
and that's my biggest fear—
losing another one,
like it would make me
even more miserable.

If my pounding heart could speak, it would say how fast it's racing—
as fast as a jet plane headed towards war
and I need paradise.
I need it. I never had a childhood.
Ever since I was little, it's just been war, war, war.

My heart is pumping fast to the promise land—
heaven, where my loved ones are.
But I just need you
to walk me through it.

MY OTHER HALF
BY A YOUNG PERSON AT CCFJC

If you had asked me to understand why
you always had to go back and forth,
I would have

If you had asked me to change
the way that I was moving
when you were still here,
I would have

Sometimes I think I drag death around like a chain

And if only I could have made my jail time less
and were able to be there for you
I would have

It's just that being left behind time after time
feels like I'm just floating
and there's nothing around me,
no way to know if things have changed or not

My eyes are too bleary to see our old memories,
and the last time I seen your face,
if only I could see you again

If I could hear you say, Brother—
I'm waiting for you while you're in there,
it would make time go by faster

THE MISSING PUZZLE PIECE
BY A YOUNG PERSON AT CCFJC

I am painting my self-portrait.
For this work I have chosen
the colors of green and red.

The green stands for my happiness,
like money.

The red for my anger,
being at a bad place in my life.

The background of my self-portrait
will have the Space Needle
because my life has been full of rainy days
and sad moments—
real moments.

In my self-portrait, I will be holding my daughter
because I love her
and she is the most important thing in my life.

In my self-portrait, my eyes will look like joy
like being in the moment—
connected.

When people see my self-portrait, I think they will say,
He's a good father,
I understand him,
He's a leader.

I would like to give my self-portrait to my baby's mom
because she appreciates the way I feel.

The title of my self-portrait will be
The Missing Puzzle Piece.

CURIOSITY
BY A YOUNG PERSON AT CCFJC

Children ask why
Teenagers question rules
Adults question life
And our elders question the past

What does that make me
if I think
about all 4?

Does that make me
a toddler
attempting to walk?

Does that make me
a rebellious son?

Does that make me
a bumbling college student?

Or does it make me
a senile old fool?

What happens
when you throw a rock
at the wall
of the ISS?*

What happens
if you go to war
for the right reasons,
but the actions
are towards the wrong cause?

And what happens
when you're a 17-year-old mixed kid
struggling to find a place
in the world
where they tell you
"find your people"
and you don't have "your people"?

And the only source of hope
you have
is the one-in-a-million chance
that you find somebody
like you?

What happens then?

---

* International Space Station.

LOOKING OUT THE WINDOW WHILE DRIVING
BY A YOUNG PERSON AT CCFJC

As I grew older, life was like riding in a car
with trees rushing by.
There was so much to see,
like people coming and going
thru my childhood.

Life rushed by far too quickly
and before I knew it,
I had left places behind,
like my first backyard
where we played football.

There are people I wish I could see again,
like my grandma that's in Mexico.

When I think of her, I miss conversations
I had with her.

There are some things I don't miss.
It's hard to think about being with my baby-momma drama.

Looking out the window, I think about where I'm headed.
I wonder if I can achieve my goals,
like spending time with my baby.

I wonder what obstacles there might be along the way—
prison.

Looking about the window while driving,
though my past is along for the ride,
there's also my destination, my future where
I'm being a father for my daughter,
providing her with
my knowledge.

DEAR MOM
BY A YOUNG PERSON AT CCFJC

I just thought you should know what I'm doing now.

I was a lost person.
Recently I've spent a lot of time
thinking about my past
and how I was messing up.
I was distant.

I am happy and nervous
for this new phase
of success.
I'm looking forward
to seeing you happy
and for me to be home.

Since the last time I saw you,
I have grown
and changed
so much.

Now I am more considerate
on how other people feel
and how I make other people feel.
I'm trying to be
more careful.

I just thought that you should know
what I wish for the future.
I hope
that one day
I can be
home with you again
with everything alright.

I am going to be trying really hard
not to mess up again.

CENTRAL DISTRICT
BY A YOUNG PERSON AT CCFJC

I'm from a street called Jackson Street
where there's a chicken spot where everybody goes
and where you can smell the JoJos frying and cooking—
smells delish! And you can hear people talking
about the block—
how it's going and how we used to live
and how the black people used to stay there.
It's a home.
Our community.
We stay strong.

On the street called Jackson Street, it used to be fun.
Great. Especially the Red Apple.
But they destroyed that.
The Barbershop? They destroyed that too.
I used to get my hair cut there,
used to see my friends, and say what's up to 'em.
I used to see my little brother get his hair cut,
say what's up to 'em, and play with 'em—a little football
or just rough him up.
I used to go to Bailey Gatzert and see all my friends, having fun.
I went to field trips. We did a lot of stuff.
When school was over, I'd see my big brother.
We used to go the field and play a little football.
Jackson Street used to be home.

White people moved us out the hood
and we had to relocate.

I was mad. Mad because I couldn't
go through the Central District.
Mad because I couldn't see my friends,
with everybody relocating to different places—
to Renton, to Kent, to Federal Way—
not able to afford homes
in the Central District.
It was like we all split up into pieces.
The Central District is different.
It's a lot of changes.
Everything is getting destroyed
and getting rebuilt.

But we still have our community there—
our black power, our families,
our ancestors, everything—our love.
We still have marches at Garfield.
We all come together
and we fight for what's right.
We are tired of seeing black people getting killed.
We just want freedom.
We are tired of seeing black kids getting locked up.
And when we're together,
we create power,
we create love,
we create strength
and a home.

A REVOLUTION FOR YOU AND ME
BY A YOUNG PERSON AT CCFJC

When there's change in the air, smelling like fresh cut lawn
or grandma's fresh cooking,
I think it might be time for a revolution.

A revolution for myself would look like a young man
spreading his knowledge
with others who need it most.

Thinking about change like this, reminds me of the time
when Barack Obama got out the White House
cuz there was no role model—nobody.
All we had was a president who only cares about himself.
So we had to make a change ourselves
by stepping up, loving one another, and accepting who we are.

A revolution to my friends and family
would have to be a peaceful marching, peaceful gathering,
a peaceful speech that tells the whole world
about the ones that been hurt the most
and been held back by the justice system—a bulldozer,
for our hopes, and our children's guidance.

A revolution for this country
would have to mean a bigger picture—non-violence,
spreading the love, spreading knowledge,
helping feed one another, heal one another.

A revolution for us could be positive
if we all have the right mindset, with no irrational mind.
Rather a wise mind than weak one
with somebody that's not afraid to speak
when they're told not to.
Or the revolution could go bad
if we're all just angry and upset about the past.
But I know, in this revolution, I'll be a better man.

Dedicated to my family

REFLECTIONS FROM PONGO MENTORS

"Youth come to us carrying profound traumas and prolific dreams. Already poets, many have never experienced the transformative, healing power of their own words. When they open up and share, we try to hold their stories to help them see their beauty, believe in their abilities, protect their hearts and preserve their hopes for a bright and free future."

– PAIGE REISCHL

"At the Patricia Clark Child and Family Justice Center, each hall features a high-walled outside area with room enough for a quarter-sized basketball court. No trees are tall enough to be seen from the inside. The winter's wet makes the ground too slippery to go outside. Birds that alight in the courtyards cannot generate enough lift to fly out.

The most surprising thing I've learned from working with youth writing poetry, is how powerful the moment is when a writer or mentor shares a very personal poem and hears their peers giving them props for saying something true and real. It humanizes everyone in the room.

– MARK JOHNSON

Pongo's fill-in-the-blank writing activity

Where I Come From

The poems, "Where I'm From" (page 48), "Where I am From" (page 68), and "Central District" (page 84), were all inspired by and written with the help of using Pongo's fill-in-the-blank writing activity on the following page.

Activity Instructions:

Sometimes the easiest way to express who we are is by describing ourselves in terms of the places, people, values, and experiences that we come from. Fill in the blanks in the poem activity. Use the words suggested or choose your own words to communicate your thoughts as clearly and powerfully as you can. Feel free to add lines of your own, to remove lines, or to change words to fit your purpose.

Pongo's Fill-in-the-Blank Writing Activity

I'm from a street where _____

_____

I'm from faith in _____

I'm from a long line of people who _____

_____

I'm from confusion about _____

I'm from laughter over _____

I come from _____

I'm from love, and I know that because _____

_____

I'm from fear, especially when I think about _____

_____

I come from a long line of _____

I come from experiences like _____

_____

I come from _____

And I wish my life would become _____

_____

That's where I'd like to be from. A place where _____

Activity Copyright © 2011 Richard Gold

STAYING STRONG

ECHO GLEN CHILDREN'S CENTER

Snoqualmie, WA
Spring 2022–Spring 2024

The Echo Glen Children's Center is a juvenile rehabilitation center for youth. Pongo has provided trauma-informed poetry workshops for youth detained at the facility since 2022.

ECHO GLEN

107
YOUTH SERVED

The poems included in this section were written by youth during Pongo programming between the spring of 2022 and spring 2024.

• • • • • • • • •

99%
OF YOUTH WRITERS ENJOYED THE PONGO WRITING EXPERIENCE

• • • • • • •

99%
of youth writers were proud of their poetry

81%
INTEND TO WRITE MORE DURING FUTURE LIFE DIFFICULTIES

UNSPOKEN IDEAS
BY A YOUNG PERSON AT Echo Glen

I wanna write about my family.
I wanna write about being here,
Echo Glen.
I wanna write about being homeless.
I wanna write about growing up.
I wanna write a poem about MMIW.*
I wanna write about my culture.
I wanna write about being overwhelmed with emotions.
I wanna write about being incarcerated and being in and out of rehab.
I wanna write about my biological parents.
I wanna write about freedom.
I wanna write about grief and loss.
I wanna write about the voice inside my head.

Dedicated to all the kids who struggle silently

---

* Missing and Murdered Indigenous Women.

WHERE I COME FROM
BY A YOUNG PERSON AT ECHO GLEN

I'm from a street where kids kill kids
and the good die young and the baddest survive.

I'm from faith in my community, my people.

I'm from a long line of people who fight
to survive and who don't have nothing.

I'm from confusion about how the same people
who we call our family, the same people we call our friends,
would be the first people to hurt us.

I'm from where people laugh about pain,
struggle and hurt because they don't wanna
embrace it and actually face the problem.

I come from struggle,
I come from pain,
and a lonely household.

I'm from love, and I know that
because no matter the problems
I've caused, and the situations I've been in,
they still got love for me at the end of the day.

I'm from fear, especially when I think about
the way I lost friends and the way
that my brother died.

I come from a long line
of hard workers and hustlers.

I come from experiences like
moms working three jobs
and kids having to take care of kids
and nobody to come home to.

And I wish my life would become
less struggles, more family,
and no worries.

That's where I'd like to be from.

A place where kids don't kill kids
and parents take care of their children,
and we don't have to spend our whole day
worrying about who's going to do something
to us and why.

WHERE I AM
BY A YOUNG PERSON AT ECHO GLEN

Locked up in my cell
That's my life right now
Been here for about a month-and-a-half
Got a 6–8-month sentence,
which is baby time to me
I live my life for the moment
I don't live a month ahead,
week ahead, day ahead
I only live for the present, like right now
People see me as criminal and label me
as someone who's a delinquent,
who won't change
That's why there's nothing
better for them to do
but throw me in a cell
For me, life's more
than just being in a cell
It's learning from your mistakes
and not making them again
so you don't come back
to where I am right now
It's about my family
My kid is due in 3 weeks
And making sure when I'm released
back into society
that I can be a father figure to my kid
My goal is to be a father
for my kid because growin' up
with no father, I ain't had a lot
So what I'm trying to say is
I'm going to break the cycle
and be there for my kid
no matter what life throws at me

I AM
BY A YOUNG PERSON AT ECHO GLEN

Today I am a raindrop
When it's early in the morning
And raindrops are sitting on the grass
Yesterday I was
At school, in cottage, then bed
On the street I am
Kinda just there
Not really standing out
Specifically to anybody or anything
Just kinda there
In my room I am constant
Thoughts of memories
To my mom I am
A boy in orange
To my father I am
The one following footsteps
I don't really know
What my friends think anymore
It's been five months
Since I've seen any of them
And I'm not the same person
I was back then
I'm not the same person
I was when I got locked up
Nearly
Really I am
A vertical shadow
When the sunset hits the trees

THE THINGS YOU GO THROUGH IN LIFE
BY A YOUNG PERSON AT ECHO GLEN

There's no friends and
No respect.
You can't soar with chickens
If you want to be an eagle.
It's like saying, do I want
To be a lowlife or highlife?
There's all these sacrifices to
Be made to have better things.
You have to surround yourself with
Positive people, not negative people.
Life is like a game, but you can't
Gain another life.
Is it worth it to be a thug and
Get mugged?
There's lows and highs in life,
But you can never give up.
Hard things in life come once
And you always gotta take it.
The easy things are not as
Valued as the hard things.
When you're locked up
Behind the cells, all those
Friends, girlfriends, and family
That you thought loved you
Aren't there for you no more.

It's like saying you think your
Homeboys are there for you,
But would they go to court, or
Would they even come visit you?
Would they put money on your books?
Your loved one is your mother because
She makes sacrifices for you.
The real evil is you. Cause whether
You are in a gang or not, you always
Make the right decision or the wrong
Decision. Being responsible is
Taking care of your loved ones and
Keeping it trucha for the ones that you hate.
Respect is not given, but
You earn it. Whether you give respect or
Earn it, you always keep it.
Having respect and responsible things
Is hard in many ways, but it's given by God.
It shows that you are responsible and manly
Enough to take care of your own lows in life.

STORY OF MY LIFE
BY A YOUNG PERSON AT ECHO GLEN

My lifestyle is based on trying to better myself
And the people around me
I think about what I'm going to become
I think about not going back to how I used to be
Like being broke
Because that had me do things I wouldn't usually do
I would do what was necessary to get money
To provide for myself and help my mom
Regardless of whether or not I hurt people
I've hurt people in the past
I regret hurting my mom the most
She was trying to provide a better lifestyle for me
I wish I was a better son
I am working on my rights and wrongs
Learning day by day in detention
I know I'm more patient than when I came in here
I used to get annoyed easily
Now I control my anger
By ignoring the subject
This is how I'm trying to change my lifestyle

WALK ONE MILE...IN MY SHOES
BY A YOUNG PERSON AT ECHO GLEN

I want you to walk one mile,
Just one, in my shoes.

I want you to know what it's like
When a person is incarcerated in the system.

I want you to know how I feel
When I'm surrounded by four white walls.

I want you to understand my pain
When I can't see my family,
I feel like I'm the victim.

I want you to walk one mile,
Just one, in my shoes.
I want you to see the beauty in my life.

I want you to know how I express myself.
My words are like bullets from a gun
That'll make you fall.

I want you to know my heart.
My love is like a needle in a haystack,
It's hard to find.

I want you to walk one mile,
Just one, in my shoes.

Then maybe you'd understand how I got here.

TEACHING ME AND MY BROTHERS TO SWIM
BY A YOUNG PERSON AT ECHO GLEN

I was born the black sheep of the family,
immediately born into the system,
dropped in the ocean, expected to swim
when I didn't know how to.

My mom tried her hardest to make my life
as perfect as could be. But somehow
I still ended up doing time here.

Everyone wants to have someone to be their own.
A friend, boyfriend, family. But somehow
I still feel alone.

I feel like I've been blindfolded,
trying to complete my time,
only being able to hear, but not to see.

I feel like a disappointment to my family and my son,
missing out on milestones because of my actions.
I wish I could go back in time, but I can't.
All I can do is take it one day at a time.

So, until the day me and my brothers walk out
these gates, God, please listen to my pleas.
I want my family and my son to be proud of me.

Help me during the next fourteen years
to be strong. I don't want my son to get used to
visiting his mom and uncles in prison his whole life.

Until me and my brothers touch down,
help me finally learn how to swim
in this ocean I was thrown into,
and help me to teach my brothers too.

I feel like even if we succeed, the world
will always try to drown us, but we know
how to swim now, even if we're still handcuffed.

Dedicated to my brothers and my son

RUNNING
BY A YOUNG PERSON AT ECHO GLEN

When I was REALLY LITTLE,
life was simple. I didn't have a lot of fear.

I wasn't afraid of things that most people were afraid of.

At the time, I ran toward video games,
kicking it with my friends,
and drinking Coca-Cola.
Life was pretty simple when I was really little.

I dreamed about being able to drink all the energy drinks
I wanted. I wanted to have more energy
to run around and play with my friends
until it was late without getting tired.

When I got a LITTLE OLDER,
I ran away from my problems.
I wanted to feel normal,
I didn't want to feel depression and anxiety.

When I ran, I expected that weed and alcohol
would solve my problems. It worked for a while.

At the time, I ran toward more drugs.
My use progressed and I started doing heroin.
That was the ultimate cure....for four to six hours,
and then there's the come down and the withdrawal.

When I ran, I hoped for my problems to go away.

TODAY when I run, I run away from the same problems,
only I don't have any drugs to help solve my problems.
Instead I have prescription medications, they help a little.

More than anything, I wish I could face my problems
and get them to go away.

TODAY when I run, I run toward
success and freedom, the ultimate goal!

More than anything, I wish I could run
to my successful future.

THOUGHTS ON PONGO FROM ECHO GLEN YOUTH

"I HAD A GOOD EXPERIENCE THE FIRST TIME I MET WITH A MENTOR. IT WAS MY FIRST TIME WRITING."

"[Pongo's] a chance to express yourself with words."

"[Pongo] helps me communicate with family, friends, and partners."

"[PONGO] MAKES ME FEEL LIKE, YOU KNOW, I'M SAYING STUFF – IMPORTANT THINGS."

"[Pongo] helps me express my feelings that I don't express to nobody."

"[Pongo's] helped my writing abilities. It helps bring more thoughts to my brain."

"[Pongo] calms me down a little bit."

"With me and my situation, I have a bit of time here. So I have a lot of emotions building up all the time. There's not much that I can do and there's not a lot of people I can talk to. So just being able to write that down on paper, and being able to say it for everybody to hear what I'm thinking all the time, and the stuff that I have to go through… we don't get opportunities like that here. Pongo let us express ourselves without any type of limits. Everybody I worked with was really nice. When mentors were talking to me, and were trying to explain to me what to do, I didn't see judgment in their eyes. They saw me as just another person."

"[Pongo] ALLOWS ME TO EXPRESS WHAT I'M FEELING."

HOW I FOUND JOY
BY A YOUNG PERSON AT ECHO GLEN

I am painting my self-portrait.
For this work I have chosen
the colors of red, blue, and rainbow.
The red stands for my frustration
from the people around me.
The people I have to go home to.
People who aren't willing to accept me
for the way that I am.
My peers don't understand
my sexuality.

The blue for my sadness from my past.
For the way that my family treated me.
The way that they wouldn't care.
I would tell them something and they didn't care.
The way that they kicked me out before.

And the rainbow stands for my confidence in myself.
Because I am proud to be the way that I am.
I am proud that I identify as my sexuality.

The background of my self-portrait will have flames
because my life has been full of drama.
Moving from foster home to foster home.
Having lots of drama going on
between my family and friends.

In my self-portrait I will be holding my cat, Fuzzy
Because joy is the most important thing in my life.
He is cuddly.
He is obedient.
He is always there for you
when you want him.

He is independent.

I can relate to the independence.
I have lived a lot of my life by myself.
Having to rely on myself.
The most important years of my life,
from eleven to fourteen.

Couch surfing.
Going from house to house.
Sleeping on the streets
outside of friends' houses.
Trespassing.
Sleeping next to someone's house.
Breaking into homes.
Going through their dog doors.
When their car isn't there,
it means they are gone.
Just so I could have a place to feel safe.

It has been ever since I was eleven-years-old.
I started hitting a rock bottom
and things were getting worse
and worse and worse.
I was kicked out
because of my sexuality.
I was adopted by my grandparents.
Six months after the adoption
they kicked me out
just because they couldn't accept
who I was and who I am.
The joy makes things disappear,
like a distraction.

It keeps my mind busy
so I don't reflect on the past
and why I was where I was.
When I was on the streets,
the joy would get rid of that thought.

In my self-portrait, my eyes
will look like fire.
All the times that I felt like
just yelling at people.
Wanting to relieve my frustration.
Made me make bad decisions.
I started using drugs
because of my frustration
with my family.

When people see my self-portrait,
I hope they will say,
"That is someone who is confident in themselves."

I would like to give my self-portrait to my sister
because she appreciates the way I am
and the way I want to be.
She was the first person that was fully
accepting of who I am.
She gave me a place to live for a while.
She would provide me food.
She gave me a feeling of security.
A feeling of joy.

The title of my self-portrait will be "How I Found Joy."

MY DOG
BY A YOUNG PERSON AT ECHO GLEN

I remember I was eating cereal
And my dog was sick
And he started breathing heavy
And I told my auntie
That he was breathing heavy
And I went downstairs
And I came back up
And he was dead

The next day
We wrapped him up in a
Native blanket
And we called the cremation place
And we got him cremated

I miss my dog

RESENTMENT
BY A YOUNG PERSON AT ECHO GLEN

I can't breathe.
I try to scream
But it's hard.

I feel like I'm
Drowning in the bottom
Of a dark ocean.

Life.
Life brings nothing but pain.
Pain becomes trauma.

Trauma turns into scars and blood.
Scars are permanent.

I hate.
I hate the fact I called you father.
At the same time I'm glad.
I'm glad because CPS gave me to mom.

Mom.
Mom is who I trust.

I'll never be what you are.

Abuse.
Abuse is why I hate you.
I wanted revenge.
Revenge would help you understand my pain.

Peace.
I'm finally at peace.
I love my mom and sister.

Love.
I love them to where
I'd do anything to protect them.

Protect them from harm and from
What you have
Done and caused.

I can breathe.
Even though it
Took twelve mental
Facilities.

I.
No we.
My family is finally
At peace.

Dedicated to mom and sister and everyone

TIRED OF THE PAIN
BY A YOUNG PERSON AT ECHO GLEN

My Uncle's Death
A lot of hurt and pain
Because it just happened yesterday
A lot of anger towards his killer
I feel lost
Drained of energy
Tired of the pain

He was a loving spirit
So outgoing
Very special to me
Was a positive figure in my life

When my dad was in jail
He was like a father figure to me
Was really understanding and listened to me
Supportive and caring

A really good person
Like, why did you take him, God?
He didn't deserve what happened

Like, why do I feel so much pain?
I needed you, and you left
I feel so lost
Drained of energy
Tired of the pain

Dedicated to uncle

STAY STRONG
BY A YOUNG PERSON AT ECHO GLEN

We got to keep a strong mind,
especially in here, and a strong body
You can't let the time get to you
You just got to try and keep your head up
Stay strong
Just block out the pain and keep going
You gotta get stronger every day
or else you get weaker
Even when it gets hard,
you just got to work harder—
like hearing bad news when you're locked up
and can't do anything about it
or looking at a picture of your family
and not being able to see them
Reading the handwriting,
but not being able to hear them
Just block out the thought completely

OPEN MINDED
BY A YOUNG PERSON AT ECHO GLEN

You want an answer to the prayer that says,
Please help me I'm hurting inside.
One day, your old life simply creeps back up
To the surface reminding you of what you've been through.
Then, the future is unknown so it's a mystery—
If what already happened will repeat itself.
The future fills me with questions like:
What am I doing with my life?
Am I there for my son?
Do I have more kids?
What's in my future?
Is it a happy life?
Do I have everything and everyone I need?
Or is it a sorrowful life?
Have my loved ones passed away?
Am I too late to get involved?
I'd like to be there for my family and son
Even if they don't need me.

CHANGING WAYS
BY A YOUNG PERSON AT ECHO GLEN

No New Year's resolution for me
No crying decree
No promises, just average changes

Less time overthinking
More time exercising
Less time eating unhealthy
More time thinking positive

Not so many regrets
A few better moments
Not so many cold nights
A few more smiles

Less frowns
More silence
Less troubles
More changes

Change after all... is good
Change after all
Is all I know

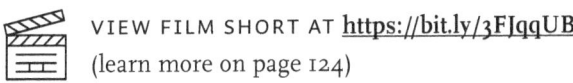 VIEW FILM SHORT AT https://bit.ly/3FJqqUB
(learn more on page 124)

DISCOVERING LOVE
BY A YOUNG PERSON AT ECHO GLEN

Perhaps love isn't what I thought.

Perhaps love isn't arguments that crash—
like angry waves on silent rocks.
Perhaps love isn't settling for glitter
when you deserve gold.
Love isn't giving yourself to someone
until there is no more you.

Perhaps love is picking yourself up
when everything seems to hold you down.
Perhaps love is finding light in yourself
when you live in a world full of dark.
Perhaps love is discovering that love we chose
in fantasies is the love we deserve within ourselves.

Love is looking in the mirror and realizing
that when we fall in love with ourselves,
it's not falling at all but rather flying.

Dedicated to myself

MY BROTHERS
BY A YOUNG PERSON AT ECHO GLEN

I'm thinking about my brothers who are locked up
And can't wait til the day we're all out
And we're all back together

It would feel like I'm safe again
It would bring joy to me to see
All of them out of jail
And hopefully they can get back on track
With life

Joy is me and all my brothers back together at the park
In the neighborhood where we'll play basketball
And do whatever we want

Feeling safe because we're all together
And we've all got each other's back
I know what my big brothers are feeling
When they're locked up
Looking at these walls

They feel the anger and the sadness
Of their time or how long they've got
Being away from their families
And the people they love the most

When they touch back down
I want to be there to support them
Until they can get back on their feet

THE JOURNEY TO THE FUTURE
BY A YOUNG PERSON AT ECHO GLEN

Impatience.
The want of not being held back
By others, by self, by the circumstances
Around you.

A better way.
A better way of living
Is what we all want
But it's hard to achieve.
It's a process of actions
And reactions, of feelings
And desires.

Second chances.
What we all deserve
But we don't all get.

Fairness.
Fairness is relative
As all of us are different
As all of us are the same.
The only question is
What is to blame.

The future.
The future isn't the end
But the journey along the way.
There's no such thing as perfection
But who cares what they say.

I'm in the journey along the way.

Dedicated to Echo Glen and the second chance it gave me

REFLECTIONS FROM PONGO MENTORS

"'Profound' is how I would describe my Pongo experience. It's been humbling to meet youth who, despite difficult circumstances, remain resilient and hopeful. Humbling, too, their trust in me—trust that somehow conjures a feeling of responsibility. It's been a privilege to sit with them as they worked bravely to express themselves; magical to see them realize their words were turning into poetry; and a joy to hear them read their poems out loud to staff and volunteers and peers. Every bit of it has been a blessing."

– MICHAEL BARRETT

"Pongo opens space to participate in the full complexity of human being. The young people I wrote with had lived lives that held profound despair and irreducible hope. Pongo allows both to exist simultaneously, coming alongside each young person to witness and honor how they make sense of their experiences. Listening with an open heart also changes the listener. The courage these young writers demonstrated in trusting me with their stories will stay with me forever. For me, Pongo's process is ultimately about offering belonging, which is transformative for all participants."

– LYLLI SRYGLEY-MEREDITH

PONGO'S FILL-IN-THE-BLANK WRITING ACTIVITY

Running

The poem, "Running" (page 104), was inspired by and written with the help of using Pongo's fill-in-the-blank writing activity on the following page.

Activity Instructions:

The purpose of this exercise is to describe the things you've run away from and the things you've run toward in your life. These things may be people, problems, feelings, ideas, etc. Fill in the blanks in the poem activity. Use the words suggested or choose your own words to communicate your thoughts as clearly and powerfully as you can. Feel free to add lines of your own, to remove lines, or to change words to fit your purpose.

Pongo's fill-in-the-blank writing activity

When I was REALLY LITTLE, I ran away from _____
(monsters under my bed, people fighting, ???)

I was afraid of _____
(being swallowed up, being left alone, ???)

At the time, I ran toward _____
(my favorite hiding place in a closet, my mom, ???)

I dreamed about _____
(a superhero's protection, ice cream, ???)

When I got a LITTLE OLDER, I ran away from _____
(bullies, my grandma's illness, ???)

When I ran, I expected that _____
(that I couldn't win, that I'd have to fight to save myself, ???)

At the time, I ran toward _____
(friends on the streets, lots of food, my dad, ???)

When I ran, I hoped for _____
(friendship, escape, money, ???)

TODAY when I run, I run away from _____
(my legal problems, bad influences, ???)

More than anything I wish I could run from _____
(my past, my friends, my dreams, ???)

TODAY when I run, I run toward _____
(my imagination, the streets, my future, ???)

More than anything I wish I could run to _____
(my freedom, to California, ???)

Activity Copyright © 2010 Shira Hasson-Schiff

YOUTH POETRY FILM SHORTS

In 2021, Pongo established a partnership with Lindy Boustedt, founder of the Screenwriting for Healing, Self-Actualization, Redemption, and Empathy (S.H.A.R.E) program. S.H.A.R.E. is a program where screenwriting and filmmaking are used as a redemptive tool for incarcerated communities around the state of Washington that might not otherwise have a voice.

Through S.H.A.R.E., Lindy worked with students at the Echo Glen Children's Center to transform select Pongo youth poems into short films; one of those poems—"Changing Ways" (page 117)—is included in this section.

WE INVITE YOU TO WATCH THAT SHORT FILM AT THE FOLLOWING LINK:
https://bit.ly/3FJqqUB

WHERE TO FROM HERE

WELL-VERSED

Online
2020 - 2024

Well-Versed: Pongo Poets Online is our online poetry submission program, through which we make writing activities available for free on our website, invite youth to submit poems, and respond to each young person with feedback and encouragement.

345 YOUTH SERVED

The poems included in this section were written by youth through our Well-Versed program between 2020 and 2024.

519 POEMS WRITTEN

27 COUNTRIES

U.S. STATES 34

AN INCOMPLETE PUZZLE
by Alexander, 2022 Well-Versed Honoree

In the world, we're all connected—
Like a jigsaw puzzle
Everything, a piece in the grand mosaic
Connected to everything
Everything playing an important role only it can
But I feel I've been placed in a spot where I don't truly fit
While others' differences are more defined and told,
I sit alone in life—
Burdened, alone

My colors slightly match—
The blue shaded like my surrounding pieces
And at first glance, my tabs and blanks fit right in
But in my forced placement, I've been botched and defaced
Where I once had perfectly fresh curves and intricacies
Has been replaced with wrinkles in my incomplete image,
And distortions where I should connect

Maybe I was printed poorly
My imperfections have been fixed,
To set me in my perfect place
But maybe I've just been placed wrong—
Criminally deformed

Now, even if I were to find my perfect place—
Interconnecting with my surroundings,
No need for accommodation from me or them—
I wouldn't fit
The wrinkles and damage still prevalent in my piece—
I can now fit nowhere

Not where intended—
As I would ruin my surroundings

And not where forced—
As the knowledge of being misplaced
would be unbearable

FONT PERSONA
BY GRAY, 2020 WELL-VERSED HONOREE

I see nothing but the average
in place of where the outstanding stood.

I've read enough to see the story before it happens
and I crave variation.

I grow tired of my own collection of masks
for the strap is growing tighter
and the polystyrene is starting to feel of flesh.

Graphite etchings act as cheap therapy.

The radio plays ballads from an age that was once,
an inch away from my fingertips
yet I already have grasped.

The members of my clique are as real to each other
as to me
as real to outsiders
as their own shadow.

My own empty hand caresses my shoulder with a sweet
gingerly touch
while the other claws at my back
and my face twists in sensual
sadistic pleasure.

And they both embrace me
in the most sincere way
until they're driven away
by the necessity of a capsule
and I forget they ever existed.

A boy in a bamboo forest once told me
I was one f***** up kid.
I took his word for it.

A girl once hurt me
and I couldn't find it in myself to hurt her back.
And I was furious about it.

These words without a face
are most likely destined to be read as riddles
and cryptic ciphers by most.

I understand them though
even if I wish with all my heart and soul
that I didn't.

And since they say this happens to everyone
I feel like I should be able to cope.

But I can't cope.

And maybe there is one more
who I can invite to my pity party
and maybe they'll get it.

I wish I could meet you

because now you've met me.

UNSPOKEN WEIGHT
by Nonhlanhla, 2024 Well-Versed Honoree

nobody ever talks about the feeling:
the loneliness that lingers in a crowded room,
the ache of never being truly understood,
the exhaustion of constantly convincing others you're genuine.

but most of all,
the feeling after you relapse,
the weight that crushes you as you lie on the floor,
wondering what's wrong with you.

wondering why you can't allow yourself to be happy,
why you'll always believe you're not enough.

the feeling that comes from shutting everyone out,
because being yourself feels like a curse.

when your facade shatters, leaving pieces in your hands,
when you swallow the words I don't care
and they settle like stones in your stomach.

SWAN LAKE
BY SRIHARINI, 2022 WELL-VERSED HONOREE

Pangs of sorrow deep inside
Hurls waves of despair
Buried deep for so long
Spirals out of control

Will the stormy seas crash?
Waiting for the rough winds
To turn into a soft gentle breeze
Time lost can never be regained

Yet the moment of silence
We all hope to calm
The darkness within us
Unknown to all except the one

The anger and pain in our eyes
When did it all begin?
The moment of truth
Will put us to rest

On mounds of crystal sand
Where we lay on our eternal
Slumber eyes wide and closed
Taking our last breath on paradise

SHELL
BY CHARLENE, 2021 WELL-VERSED HONOREE

A shell sitting here
A meat mesh suit
Nothing more, everything less
A shell
Devoid of occupants
Of emotion, empathy, and sympathy
Only one remains
In a lonesome chair
Apathy

Twist, conform, hide
Her eyes swivel around
The raven swivels its head
Beady little eyes tracking every movement
There is no time for rest
For there is no safety

Danger
Visible, invisible
She mutters to herself
Paranoid, hurt, scared
What is there to be
Except none

I feel nothing
And yet
I am alive
Nothing left
But a shell to die
A facade made to thrive

Wings flutter restlessly
Eyes dart around on alert
Ears pricked up
For the shot of the gun

For there is none
In the field of some
None who truly understand me
Only some who care about me

And yet
I walk
On the yellow brick road
To the land of Kansas
With oil and grease

In hope
Of receiving a real heart
One capable of seeing,
Healing and feeling
Easily said and not done
The road stretches afar

I am on my way

MYSELF: REVISED EDITION
BY Kalah, 2020 Well-Versed Winner

I am revising myself, an improved edition
The new version will say something about forgiving myself
for trying to change someone for the better
when all they wanted was to ruin
my hopes and dreams for the future

Chapter 1 would highlight the benefits of loving myself
I need to show kindness to myself
by telling myself that it is okay to love how I look or think
I need to mend myself by letting go of all the pain and trauma
from my unforgettable childhood
I'd call this chapter, The Beginning of a New Chance

Chapter 2 would explore how my mistakes
have also been my teachers
I made a mistake when I trusted someone so deeply
that when they left, they exposed all my deepest secrets
But I learned that people will do anything
to see you fail and crumple
I'd titled this chapter, Never Fear Change

In another chapter, I'd talk about
how I want to toss some things out of my life
Like the day that my mother struck me
first with a bat and then
with her fist, leaving a busted mouth full of blood
as I caught the city bus to get help
and never returned to her care and instead
was put into foster care for the best

Definitely, the last section will describe my many aspirations
My aspirations are to become someone in life
so I can prove my mother wrong and show her
what she had lost when she decided to abuse me
My aspirations are the colors of baby blue and rose gold
And they look like a new beginning for my life as an adult
which is soon to come

I REMEMBER
BY AAMUKTHA, 2024 WELL-VERSED HONOREE

Being 11 years old
The cacophonous chords from the radio as the car
(breaks the silence, then reluctantly returns it)
Zooms past me full of boys
(acting their age by pretending to be older)
Yelling out to me
I turn and look

My vision blurs as I walk the rest of the way home

I never wanted to crawl out of my skin more
I remember
The first time I felt
Like I could be an object of someone's gaze
All the pieces of me that
Were supposed to make up a human
Could be picked apart
For a feature film
For spectators behind
Tinted windows
Who could give me their hurt
And not feel a thing

WHAT THEY WERE WEARING
by Vixen, 2023 Well-Versed Honoree

Hand prints painted along their clothing,
Their bodies, their hair.
Although never showing,
The burn of the memories is still there.

The betraying touch of a friend,
Burning against her skin.
"Never tell anyone," they said
For defilement is surely a sin.

"Don't lie," they said as he cried out with vulnerability.
"You could've fought back," they said as he froze in his fears.
For he was bigger, stronger, had the capability.
So how could he have been so weak
As to "let" someone do that, they whispered,
As he drowned in his own tears.

"He wouldn't do something like that," everyone protested
When they finally spoke about what happened.
"Why didn't you tell anyone?" everyone questioned
When she kept it to herself.
"That can't happen to men," everyone denied
As his flashbacks summoned.

"Maybe you provoked them," they said, as if it were any excuse.
"You should have tried harder," they tried to pin the blame
On the one who was hurting.
"It's your fault," they told the abused.
"After all... what were you wearing?"

I JUST THOUGHT YOU SHOULD KNOW

BY ARIA, 2020 WELL-VERSED HONOREE

I just thought you should know what I'm doing now.
I am your resilient daughter,
one of the 7 who you raised to be fearless,
who spends a lot of time caring for others
but forgetting oneself.

I just thought you should know how I'm feeling.
I am peaceful because I'm surrounded by people who love me.
I just thought you should know what I've been through.
Since your last breath, right after I said goodbye,
I have grown wiser as you promised I would.

Our Sunday night phone calls were significant to me,
especially now, when you can no longer answer.

I just thought you should know what I wish for the future.
I hope that I become the warrior you once were.
There are battles fought on the ground
and others deliberated by the Spirit.
The battle rages on.

I just thought you should know
I am glad I don't have to worry
about your health anymore
or if you would remember me.

I just thought you should know what I miss a lot.
I miss the way we used to talk on the phone
or sit in the most peaceful silence.
I just thought you should know that I learned
how to hold my peace,
fight with love, pray without ceasing,
and uphold grace from wherever I stand.
Thank you, Dad, for loving me
in a way to teach us all
how to love.

A POEM ABOUT A DEAD GIRL
by Maya, 2024 Well-Versed Honoree

growing up
i was the kid who played in cemeteries
who visited them over spring break
who spent birthdays at burials

growing up
i was the kid
who ate cupcakes atop of graves
who left flowers on top of tombs
who walked around looking for gifts to give to Her
i grew up
burying race cars under a tree for Her
eating apricots every summer for Her
looking for messages in our toy trains from Her

i grew up with
Her name in their mouths
Her name in my name
Her name in our wifi passwords

i grew up with Her name
and Her ghost
i grew up with Her
and she didn't get to grow up with us

i grew up
hearing stories about Her
how she was born and
how she left
how she played basketball with my dad

i grew up
hearing about
how Her birthday decorations were left up
how Her favorite foods were
pizza and mashed potatoes
how on Her last day she wouldn't eat pizza
i grew up
hearing stories about Her
how my mom spent the night sleeping on Her grave
how my dad woke up looking for Her
how my mom sat in a bathtub with a blade
waiting for the perfect moment
i think she might still be waiting

i grew up
being told
we don't write stories about dead Girls
well here's a story about a dead Girl

Happy birthday, SR

THOUGHTS ON PONGO FROM WELL-VERSED YOUTH

"AT A TOUGH POINT IN MY LIFE – WHEN I FELT VOICELESS– PONGO CAME ALONG LIKE A TOUCH OF REASSURANCE. IT GAVE ME A PLACE TO START OVER; A MEGAPHONE TO SHOUT THROUGH. IT'S HELPED ME BUILD MY IDENTITY UP FROM THE GROUND AND NOW MY VOICE FEELS HEARD AND VALUED."

- KUSUMITA, 2021 PONGO POETRY PRIZE WINNER

"Coming across Pongo has been an experience that I could only describe as transformative, opening my eyes to the power of words in addressing real-world issues. I have found courage in shedding light on struggles often left unspoken in today's world. I am deeply grateful to Pongo for giving me the platform to not only nurture my creativity but also give me a chance to speak on an important societal challenge."

– SAMAH, 2024 PONGO POETRY PRIZE WINNER

"Pongo poetry writing made me feel a sense of belonging and relief. I've never received such encouraging & personalized feedback before Pongo; this made me feel seen and inspired me to keep writing and sharing more personal stories.

The poem I wrote was from the perspective of my younger self attempting to process the domestic abuse me and my family survived at the hands of my biological father. This was the first time I put my very personal experience in a poem and for that, I thank Pongo for helping me step out of my comfort zone."

– CLEMENCE, WELL-VERSED WRITER

"I was amazed by my writing, seeing it so long after I first reflected on the loss of my father to Parkinson's Disease and Alzheimer's. We lost him long before he was gone, sadly. He suffered so much, and we continued to say goodbye every time. I had forgotten how profound it was for me to write this poem when so many of my feelings were sheltered beforehand. There is such power in our words, and the chance to transfer that power to a page makes writing a treasure for life—a gift that cannot be taken away. There's a form of healing found in writing. I pray that the healing I have found from scripting words to life will impact every person who reads them."

– ARIA, 2020 WELL-VERSED HONOREE

"I THINK WRITING CAN SOMETIMES BEGIN TO FEEL VERY ACADEMIC AND STALE FOR TEENAGERS, AND CHANGING THAT NARRATIVE FOR MYSELF THROUGH POETRY HAS BEEN VERY RELIEVING. I AM GRATEFUL PONGO RECOGNIZES THAT, AND HAS FOSTERED A COMMUNITY OF PEOPLE WITH SIMILAR THOUGHTS TO MINE, WHICH IS INCREDIBLY INSPIRING."

– CHRISTIAN, 2022 PONGO POETRY PRIZE WINNER

"Since I can remember poems have been an outlet for me to express my deepest thoughts, and finding a way to configure those thoughts is a great passion of mine. I feel that everyone needs to have an outlet like this, it could be art, academics, sports, or anything you feel passionate about."

– JOHNNY, 2023 PONGO POETRY PRIZE WINNER

WHERE TO FROM HERE?
by Pontsho, 2023 Well-Versed Honoree

My space
My color
My mind
My heart breaks into thin pieces,

wrapped with nothing but hurt
I cry but still no hope

Where to from here?

When no one is around and willing
to give one a place to hide their sorrows?

Where to from here when my space
is your space for your inferior?

Where to from here when my color
is mistaken for the past and discrimination?

Where to from here when I can't speak
my mind because hate will take place and lead?

Tell me where to from here

when one tries so hard to reach out
they get punished for being true?

This life we living turned out into mixed
paints that won't ever make any painting clear

So where to from here?

REALITY
By Johnny, 2023 Well-Versed Winner

Sometimes we shame people for looking
past the bright side of the moon
To peek into the darkness that slowly absorbs them
They may look like nothing is running inside of them

But in reality, they are fighting a war that cannot be won
They have fathomed that the world is not in a cycle
Each day we wonder what new animal will go extinct

We wonder where the latest school shooting happened
We wonder what state the climate will be in 20 years
We wonder when people will look past appearances and into souls
We wonder if this messed up world will ever change

When did people decide that history
should be labeled as black and white?
That history is a story

But some people don't read past the first chapter
They don't flip the page and see the suffering

They don't see the Native Americans being massacred by Columbus
They don't see the whip scars on melanated skin
They don't see the little girl forced to have a child
at 12 because he couldn't control himself

All they see is the cover
The front page of the magazine
They see a food-eating contest on the top of their feed
But don't bother to look further and see
the little boy's body slowly decaying from hunger

The reality is that the world is nothing but a narrative

What matters is the part of the book you decide to read

RICE ON A ROLLERCOASTER
By Noah, 2023 Well-Versed Honoree

water simmering,
hair blowing out the window,
radio playing and i don't know
how to say this any better,
but i'm FREAKING OUT
about so many things that i don't know
how to describe about consciousness and evolution
and if some psycho is just programming
everything in my world, but even if that's happening
then it's still my world,
but if it's our world
then why are we messing it up so badly?
then the radio puts on a story about palestine
and genocide and hostages
and from the river to the sea
and why do i have a right
to think about these deep questions
when kids my age are being kidnapped,
then bombed, hollowed out, and by the way
the fireflies are dying and so are the butterflies
and the bees and birds and everything i care about
and maybe i'm just being naive
for thinking that planting a few oaks
can fix everything but what else can,
some bill that never gets passed
until they're already gone,

then my mind switches back
to complexity and entanglement
and why did my grandma give us
the 101 plastic cookie cutters
that we don't need and are just exacerbating
our planet's stress and why are we so fixated
on what present santa's going to get us for christmas
when we don't even know if we have free will
or why we exist or if there's god;
maybe we're like the rice in the pot,
just going along for the ride.

WHAT WE CARRIED
by Victoria, 2024 Well-Versed Honoree

If an immigrant
chooses to leave behind
everything they know
what do they carry?

My parents said the clothes on their backs
My sisters said hope in their hearts
I carry the weight of their sacrifice
I carry the feeling of being lost

If my roots are in Russia
but I was born in the land of the free
what does that make me?
What do I carry?

I carry a childhood where I could speak my mind
I carry curiosity about a place of wonder
but also a place of violence and fear
a place where people don't have a voice

Childhood books filled with the Cyrillic alphabet,
old cassette tapes of Soviet pop stars—
collect dust in my house
as I think about the definition of identity

If I knew who I was, I would be able to tell you
but the words don't come to mind
all I see is what my family left behind
All I know is what they did for me

If this is who I am, a person seeking answers,
I might be searching all my life
in the mirror, in others' faces, in old photos
reaching out for an understanding that might never come

I carry gratitude for a country that nestled us
A family that had to let go of everything
to be able to hold onto their dreams
to let me question the definition of "me"

I am grateful for the things we carried

A PALESTINIAN MOTHER
by Samah, 2024 Well-Versed Winner

A Palestinian mother,
A poster for love and bravery.
The one who waits for her martyred son.
The one who weeps whilst holding her dead child.

A Palestinian mother,
A poster for resistance and courage.
The one who endures sleepless nights
from the sound of missiles above.
The one who stares at the bleak sky waiting for it to clear.

A Palestinian mother,
A poster for nurture and motherhood.
The one who starves for her children to eat.
The one who smiles softly to comfort her crying newborn.

A Palestinian mother,
The one who is killed to protect her family.

A Palestinian mother,
Humanity's symbol of hope.

WHAT IS LOVE?
by Nennin, 2021 Well-Versed Honoree

I wanna know is love like in the movies and shows,
where the world looks beautiful, like a blooming rose

I wanna know does love make your heart flutter,
where you can't speak, can't do, every thought is a sputter

I wanna know does love bring joy, happiness, pain, hurt
Is it to enjoy or is love something your eyes should avert

I wanna know if love is something to chase,
something to want, something we need

Or is love just a trap, a feeling to mislead

I wanna know is love good or bad,
euphoric or chaotic

I wanna know, what is love?

Because I seem to have forgotten

I HATE YOU OUT OF LOVE
by Maeve, 2020 Well-Versed Honoree

I hate you out of love.
I do this for you. I do this for God.
I help you. This is out of love.

I was taught to yearn for the prince of my dreams while
there sat a gorgeous princess next to me.
But the moment they saw my hand
in hand with hers
was the moment I questioned if there was a God.

They diagnosed me ill while religiously pouring holy water
onto us as if they could pray away what God made.

We buried ourselves away
fearfully hiding, fearfully loving.
Punishing our instinctual way
of natural love.

Made us believe we were wrong.
Taught how to invalidate with ease.

I declared myself a liar.
I deemed her a falsifier.

They put ashes on our forehead
but could barely touch us out of disgust.

They purged the demons
that we called our love.

I bellow out God hates me. He hates
my love. Where is this God of love
while you tear apart ours?

They reply with a smile so high,
I do this for you. I do this for God.
I help you. This is out of love.

A TASTE OF INTIMACY
by Kusumita, 2021 Well-Versed Honoree

You and me, we spread like sad fire.
We are the rustle of autumn—
The clang of metal
That cuts deep.

We are open mouthed puppets.
Our disheveled vulnerabilities
Hold hands and run.

We,
We love hard—
Like cherry red drops
Falling
To earth.

Our days echo
Between the trembling
Lands of dream and reality.

A silent statue—
We are the first stroke
Of a doomed word never penned.

Our shared name
Sits like a hymn in our chest—
Rolling about in times of dread.

You and me—
We hold, we stay,
We pen dark sagas on sand
And sketch collarbones by day.

You and me, we fall, get back up and fall again.
You and me, we are time, space and seas astray.

THOUGHTS ON PONGO FROM WELL-VERSED YOUTH

"I found Pongo after Google searching for more poetry opportunities. Pongo gave me an outlet for my writing and like many other authors, I feel that the whole point of writing is to give yourself and others an outlet for anything and everything. This poem is very special to me because it explains the frustrations on how even the most 'loving' communities are still unaccepting of the LGBTQ+community who are still faced with hateful oppression to this day."

– Maeve, 2020 Well-Versed Honoree

"Submitting my poems to Pongo and receiving a response – knowing that someone read my work – was heartwarming, and the feedback was thoughtful and personal."

– Aamuthka, Well-Versed Writer

"When I first started writing on Pongo, I thought it was a way to release all of my stress and pain. However, I did not think it would catch the eyes of numerous people in the world. I love writing for Pongo, and I cannot wait to create so many more works with Pongo Teen Writing. Thank you for letting me be free to write my heart out. Remember that when times get tough, poetry can help you through it all."

– Kalah, 2020 Well-Versed Winner

MAMBA MENTALITY VOL.2
by Trent, 2021 Well-Versed Winner

The different animal, but the same beast
Detailed
A mentality of calculated cunning
Vigorous
Talent, posture, a hunger for more
Rigorous
Defined by animosity
Patience
Driven by ferocity
Instinct
The way to live… as the Mamba lived

Amazing potential
Untapped
Visually focused, classically trained
Unrecognized
A chance at greatness
Time
A greatness achieved
Infantile
A different breed, but the same humanity
Intelligence
Dormant, but never asleep
Limitless
A view of the future
Dreamer
A passion for things to come
Joy
The way to live… as the Mambacita lived

Connected, never broken
Aligning
Taken away, but never vacant
Liveliness
Bonded by basketball
Connection
But spirits together for higher purposes
A father and daughter on the surface
Family
Courageous hunger and devotion underneath
Mastermind
The way to live
As not only the Mamba and Mambacita lived
But the footsteps and motions
The calculated nature
The mentality
We should all strive to achieve

Dedicated to Kobe and Gianna Bryant

SEVENTEEN FOREVER
by Christian, 2022 Well-Versed Winner

Honestly, I'm not ready to grow up.
I can barely put into words how scared I am.
It's like getting pushed into the deep end.
I need floaties.
I need someone to hold me.
I need someone to save me.

I'm just a kid.
I was just a baby not long ago.
I'm not ready and I'll probably never be.

I just wanna go back to the 2000s
But there is no time machine, and no button to press
So I'll deal with the rest and try to be the best
That I can be with the rest of time I have left.

If I could get one wish I'd stay seventeen forever.
I would kiss my momma goodnight every day.
I'd dance till dawn playing all my old songs.
I'd stay up past my bedtime binging 13 Reasons Why.

I just wanna stay here,
I just wanna stay seventeen forever.

Maybe I would do things differently
And maybe I would pick new friends.
I don't know what I'd do
But at least I would be safe.
I'd have a safety net that billions would cling to.

Now my mistakes seem to be counted
On the fingers of the hands of everyone
I have to appeal to.

I can't be myself.
I have to be mature, polite, strong,
and confident always.
That just isn't me.
I'm only seventeen.

PONGO'S FILL-IN-THE-BLANK WRITING ACTIVITY

I Just Thought You Should Know

The poem, "I Just Thought You Should Know" (page 138), was inspired by and written with the help of using Pongo's fill-in-the-blank writing activity on the following page.

Activity Instructions:

The purpose of this exercise is to communicate your thoughts and feelings to a person you may not see much anymore, due to life circumstances. This is a chance to say things you never had a chance to say, or to tell this important person about yourself— the challenges you have faced, the achievements you have accomplished, and how these things have made you who you are today. Fill in the blanks in the poem activity. Use the words suggested or choose your own words to communicate your thoughts as clearly and powerfully as you can. Feel free to add lines of your own, to remove lines, or to change words to fit your purpose.

Pongo's fill-in-the-blank writing activity

Dear _____ (Mom, Dad, Sister, Grandma, old friend, ???),

I just thought you should know what I'm doing now.

    I am a _____ person
               (strong, angry, happy, lonely, ???)

    who spends a lot of time _____
                     (dancing, watching movies, hanging out with my friends, ???).

I just thought you should know how I'm feeling.

    I am _____
          (happy, nervous, depressed, ???)

    because _____

I just thought you should know what I've been through.

    Since the last time I saw you, I have _____ so much
                               (grown, suffered, changed, ???)

The time that I _____ was especially important.

I just thought you should know what I wish for the future.

I hope that _____

_____

I just thought you should know what I don't miss about you.

    I am glad I don't have to worry about _____

_____ anymore.

I just thought you should know what I miss a lot.

I miss the way *(you, we)* used to _____

_____

I just thought you should know _____

Activity Copyright © 2006 Kevin Jones

ABOUT WELL-VERSED

Ann Teplick is a cherished member of the Pongo community, who has served as a youth poetry mentor, a Project Leader, a trainer, and an ambassador for our work. Every poem submitted to Pongo through Well-Versed is reviewed by Ann, who engages each piece with her characteristic thoughtfulness and careful eye, and responds to each author with her feedback and encouragement.

"I come from story. I believe each of us has important stories to tell and that art is the perfect vehicle to express them. I know when we do, we have the opportunity to better understand ourselves and our worlds. I believe when we share our stories, we open the doors for others to better understand who we are. And that this understanding opens the door to kindness and compassion. For me, elevating youth voices is critical, and especially the voices of those who may be overlooked."

— ANN TEPLICK

HOW TO GET **INVOLVED**

If reading this collection inspires you to learn more about Pongo Poetry Project and ways to get involved, we invite you to visit our website, www.pongopoetryproject.org, in order to:

- Download free writing activities
- Submit poetry
- Learn about volunteer and training opportunities
- Purchase other Pongo books
- Make a donation

www.ingramcontent.com/pod-product-compliance
Lightning Source LLC
Chambersburg PA
CBHW050328010526
44119CB00050B/721